Verdi for KIDS

Verdi
for KIDS

His Life and Music

WITH 21 ACTIVITIES

HELEN BAUER | Foreword by Deborah Voigt

CHICAGO
REVIEW
PRESS

First edition

Published by Chicago Review Press Incorporated

814 North Franklin Street

Chicago, Illinois 60610

ISBN 978-1-61374-500-7

Library of Congress Cataloging-in-Publication Data

Bauer, Helen, 1943-

   Verdi for kids : his life and music with 21 activities / Helen Bauer ; foreword
by Deborah Voigt. — First edition

         p. cm.

   Includes bibliographical references and index.

   ISBN 978-1-61374-500-7 (pbk.)

   1. Verdi, Giuseppe, 1813-1901—Juvenile literature. 2. Composers—Italy—
Biography—Juvenile literature. I. Title.

   ML3930.V4B38 2013

   782.1092—dc23

   [B]

                                     2012042742

Cover and interior design: Monica Baziuk

Front cover images: Verdi, Leemage/Getty; Il Trovatore poster, Library of
Congress; Theater, gmalandra/iStockphoto; Giuseppina Strepponi, Lebrecht
Music and Arts/Photographers Direct.

Back cover images: Piano, Library of Congress; Carnival mask, Thomas M.
Perkins/Shutterstock; La Scala, Federico Rostagno/Shutterstock.

Interior illustrations: Jim Spence

Printed in the United States of America

5   4   3   2   1

To Arona:
Continue to be the admirable person you are today.
May you always be successful and joyful
in all that you are and do.

Contents

Open my heart and you will see,
Graved inside of it, "Italy."

—Robert Browning, English poet

FOREWORD

I'M VERY HAPPY that you've chosen to pick up this book about the life of the renowned opera composer Giuseppe Verdi!

In today's 21st-century world, opera often takes a backseat to other types of music. In fact, classical music in general is rarely the option that many people, especially young people, choose to listen to.

But *oh*! What those people are missing!

Opera is full of drama and emotion, intrigue and action. It's an art form that combines live singing of the most spectacular kind with vivid acting and the playing of great music—all in one place and at one time.

One of the most important things about opera that many kids don't realize: we singers do it all *without microphones*. We study and train for years to be able to sing beautifully—not shout—over the playing of orchestras that sometimes number over a hundred pieces. Impressive, no?

Speaking of impressive, Giuseppe Verdi was one of the best of all the opera composers. His operas (he composed about 28 of them) have been performed for enthusiastic audiences for more than 170 years and are often the mainstay of many of the world's opera houses today. Even if you are completely new to opera, you would probably be surprised by how much of Verdi's music you have already heard, and do hear, in everyday life. Themes from his operas are used in movies, commercials, and celebratory events to this day, and are famous and familiar.

When I was growing up and finding that I loved to sing, singing at both my school and my church, I really had no idea that some 30 years down the road I would be one of the world's most well-known opera sopranos. At the time I didn't know anything about opera. Then one day one of my voice teachers said to me, "I think you have a voice that could sing opera!" I was thrilled; it was like being admitted into a wonderful, secret world that held untold treasures. And it does.

This is why I'm so excited for you that you've decided to pick up this book. Whether you sing or find that you have the wonderful ability to recognize and enjoy great classical music when you hear it, learning about and listening to opera is a very fulfilling and exciting experience that will continue to bring you joy for your entire life.

Welcome to the world of Giuseppe Verdi!

Deborah Voigt

NOTE TO READERS

The YEAR 2013 marks the 200th anniversary of Giuseppe Verdi's birth. Verdi not only gave us glorious operas but lived his life with devotion to his country and its people. His concerns ranged from the lofty ideals of freedom for his compatriots to compassion for the less fortunate and to the nurturing of the land. He lived through the horrible loss of his family and had to deal with the disapproving opinions of his neighbors. The composer became a national symbol of patriotism and Italian culture. Today, his operas are performed throughout the world.

From this book you will gain knowledge about Verdi's life, an understanding of Italy's revolutionary struggle, and a taste of opera that will, I hope, develop into a lasting interest that can enrich each day. Operatic and musical terms are set in bold type at their first appearance in the text and defined in a glossary in the back. Sidebars throughout expand on the people and events that touched Verdi's life, and "music notes" delve more deeply into the musical concepts introduced. The activities are fun and entertaining, and they highlight aspects of Verdi's life and times.

Viva music!

TIME LINE

1813	❖	Giuseppe Verdi is born on October 9 in Roncole, Italy, to parents Luigia and Carlo
1815	❖	Battle of Waterloo; Napoleon is defeated
1817	❖	Verdi attends elementary school
1818	❖	Starts music lessons in Busseto, Italy
1821	❖	Carbonari uprising in Naples, Italy
1822	❖	Verdi becomes organist in Saint Michael the Archangel Church in Roncole
1823	❖	Attends the Busseto *ginnasio* (secondary school)
1825	❖	Studies with Ferdinando Provesi
1829	❖	Becomes Provesi's assistant
1832	❖	Moves to Milan, Italy, and applies to the Milan Conservatory; begins private studies with Vincenzo Lavigna
1833	❖	Provesi dies; Verdi's sister Giuseppa dies
1836	❖	Verdi becomes music master in Busseto and composes *Oberto*; marries Margherita Barezzi
1837	❖	Birth of Verdi's daughter Virginia
1838	❖	Verdi resigns job as music master in Busetto; his son Icilio is born; Virginia dies.
1839	❖	Verdi moves to Milan; son Icilio dies; premiere of *Oberto* at La Scala
1840	❖	Verdi's wife, Margherita, dies; Verdi returns to Busseto; *Un giorno di regno* premieres at La Scala
1842	❖	*Nabucco* premieres at La Scala; Giuseppina Strepponi sings the role of Abigaille
1843	❖	*I Lombardi* premieres at La Scala
1844	❖	*Ernani* debuts in Venice and *I due Foscari* debuts in Rome
1845	❖	*Giovanna d'Arco* premieres at La Scala
1846	❖	*Attila* premieres in Venice
1847	❖	*Macbeth* premieres in Florence; *I masnadieri* debuts in London; *Jérusalem* premieres in Paris; Verdi and Giuseppina Strepponi move to Paris

1848	First Italian War of Independence; Verdi returns to Milan during the uprisings, buys land
1849	Rome declared a republic; Verdi returns to Busseto with Giuseppina Strepponi
1851	*Rigoletto* premieres in Venice; Verdi moves to Sant'Agata; Luigia Verdi dies
1853	Uprising in Milan; *Il trovatore* premieres in Rome; *La traviata* premieres in Venice
1859	Second Italian War of Independence; *Un ballo in maschera* premieres in Rome; slogan "Viva V.E.R.D.I." is heard; Verdi marries Giuseppina Strepponi
1860	Giuseppe Garibaldi leads an uprising in Italy
1861	Verdi is elected as a member of the first Italian Parliament
1865	Verdi resigns from Parliament
1866	Third Italian War of Independence; Verdi lives in Paris
1867	Carlo Verdi dies; Antonio Barezzi dies; Verdi returns to Italy and becomes the guardian of his great niece Maria Filomena
1869	The new Cairo Opera House opens with *Rigoletto*
1870	Franco-Prussian War begins
1871	Franco-Prussian War ends; Rome becomes the capital of Italy; *Aida* premieres in Cairo
1875	Verdi sworn in as a senator to the Italian Parliament in Rome
1876	Conducts *Aida* in Paris
1878	Maria Filomena marries
1879	Maria Filomena gives birth to a daughter
1883	Richard Wagner dies
1887	*Otello* premieres at La Scala; Verdi awarded honorary citizenship of Milan
1889	Verdi buys land to build the Casa di riposo, a rest home for elderly musicians, in Milan
1893	*Falstaff* premieres at La Scala; Verdi made an honorary citizen of Rome
1897	Giuseppina dies
1898	Verdi lives in a suite in the Grand Hotel in Milan
1899	Official opening of the Casa di riposo
1901	Verdi suffers a stroke and dies

INTRODUCTION

Italian Opera—A History
of Splendor and Beauty

*S*INCE THE EXOTIC travels of Marco Polo, the 13th-century explorer, Italians have delved into uncharted realms. Over the centuries many inquisitive Italians spent their lives investigating, researching, testing, and probing the unknown and the untried. These intelligent, curious people have made significant contributions to the arts, literature, philosophy, science, and music. In fact, the beginning of modern Western civilization can be attributed to Italians.

Reflecting their quest for knowledge, Italians founded the first European university in Bologna in 1088. The school was declared independent from the educational institutions of the church by the Holy Roman Emperor Frederick I. By the 12th century the university was attracting students and scholars from many European countries. One hundred years later the curriculum grew to include philosophy and medicine.

Rinascimento, the Italian word for rebirth, provided the name of the Renaissance—a period of about 150 years beginning in 1450 that restored an interest in learning using classical sources. The scholars of the Renaissance researched and debated literature, economics, government, science, and the arts. This rebirth began in the Italian city of Florence before spreading to other countries. The Renaissance lifted the heavy curtains that had kept Europe dark throughout the Middle Ages as great thinkers took a fresh look at the arts and sciences and stressed individual achievement, logic, and reason. Scholars sought factual scientific evidence and observed the universe and natural phenomena with open minds, which allowed them to develop new ideas and inventions. The Renaissance brought about a cultural and intellectual revival that led to many changes in Western society.

The Baroque era followed the Renaissance. Starting in 1600, this period also lasted about 150 years. The word *baroque* means elaborate and refers to the ornate style of the art, music, and architecture of the era. This movement began in Rome during a time of much tension and turmoil in Europe. Throughout the Baroque epoch all the economic, religious, educational, governmental, and scientific traditions of society were in transition.

Many of the world's most recognized artists are Italian. The Renaissance and Baroque artists created magnificent paintings and sculptures. The most famous include Michelangelo (1475–1564) and Leonardo da Vinci (1452–1519). Michelangelo was a sculptor, architect, and engineer as well as a painter. A man of many talents and interests, Leonardo da Vinci sculpted, painted, invented, and studied science.

Renaissance musicians wrote secular as well as religious works. Madrigals were secular songs in which the words of the poems were set to music. These songs were popular in the Italian courts. In the late 16th century, just as the Baroque era was starting, a group of scholars meeting in Florence were studying Greek tragedies. Known as the Florentine Camerata, this society of thinkers decided to write their own plays set to music in a manner that they believed would replicate what the ancient Greeks had employed in their plays.

The Florentine Camerata's concepts were nurtured during the Baroque era by various **composers** (those who write the music) attempting to define a method and course for this new musical genre. Jacopo Peri (1561–1633) was living in Florence when he set a play to music in 1600 as a part of the entertainment at the wedding celebration of a nobleman; his *Eurydice* is the first surviving attempt at this type of work. A contemporary of William Shakespeare, Claudio Monteverdi (1567–1643), a madrigal composer from northern Italy, is often called the father of this musical form known as **opera** (a word based on the Latin word for work). Using the Greek myth of Orpheus, Monteverdi crafted *L'Orfeo*, a creation that incorporated all the elements necessary to meet the standards that the Camerata had set, 200 years before Giuseppe Verdi's birth. Many composers followed Monteverdi's lead.

Opera began as an experiment and as entertainment for the wealthy and noble elements of the society. From this beginning opera fired up the imagination of the public. By the middle of the 17th century, cities all over Italy began to build opera houses modeled after the first one that had been built in Venice in 1637. The latest type of entertainment became ever more popular as an adoring Italian public crowded these theaters. By 1700 other countries in Europe, including Austria, France, and England, were erecting their own opera houses.

Composers outside of Italy also became interested in this innovative musical idea. The Italian-born composer Jean-Baptiste Lully (1632–1687), who worked for the French court of Louis XIV, developed operas that were more suited to the French fondness for dance by incorporating ballet into his works. The German composer George Frideric Handel (1685–1759) was captivated by the possibilities provided by this type of work. He even moved to Italy to study opera and became one of the most beloved composers of Italian opera. In Great Britain, John Blow (1649–1708) wrote the first opera in English, soon followed by *Dido and Aeneas* penned by Henry Purcell (1659–

1695), which is considered to be one of the greatest English operas.

By the beginning of the 18th century, opera was established as a magnificent form of entertainment. This was the Classical era of music, which began in about 1750 and lasted until around 1830. Toward the middle of this period the German Christoph Willibald von Gluck (1714–1787) felt that the art form needed to be improved. Gluck believed that composers and **librettists** (those who write the words to an opera) were exaggerating too much and including too many far-fetched ideas in their operas. He also thought that the singers had become more important than the music. Gluck set out to change opera. His 1762 *Orfeo ed Euridice* (Orpheus and Euridice) contained music that suited the drama, and he increased the role of the **chorus**. The Italian composer Niccolò Jommelli (1714–1774) followed Gluck's reform guidelines. His operas featured the drama and allowed fewer of the theatrical displays of the singers, thereby reducing their importance. A new direction was established by Gluck's reforms and accepted by many future composers.

During the Romantic era (1830–1920) the popularity of opera spread to many more countries. Composers from a variety of nations entered the stage with their works, which they flavored with the spices native to their own lands. In Russia Mikhail Glinka (1804–1857) composed *A Life for the Tzar*; during the same period the first American opera composer, William Henry Fry (1813–1864), was writing *Leonora*.

Throughout the decades, Italian opera retained its own identity; the pomp and splendor of the major **scenes**, the display of emotion, and the beauty of the flowing line of the Italian words set to infectious music—all are part of the Italian operatic customs and heritage. These traditions were preserved by the composers who wrote Italian operas in the early 19th century. These composers include Gioacchino Rossini (1792–1868), who wrote the comic *The Barber of Seville*; Gaetano Donizetti (1797–1848), composer of the heartbreaking *Lucia di Lammermoor*; and Vincenzo Bellini (1801–1835), best known for his tragic drama *Norma*. They left a generous legacy and set the stage for their successors.

Operatic works, whether written as a drama or a comedy, attract and fascinate their audiences. The emotional power of the music, the magnificent voices, the splendor of the scenery, and often the special effects, all combine to create a certain magic. There is extraordinary excitement floating in the air of an opera house just as the curtain starts to rise…

What does an Ethiopian princess enslaved in Egypt have in common with a scheming, stout knight? What is the link between a gypsy and a court jester? They are all characters in operas composed by Giuseppe Verdi, who dominated Italian opera for 50 years and brought the art form to its greatest heights. ❧

Verdi *for* KIDS

A Quiet Child

1813–1831

*"If music is central to a person's life, it can be
something very special and life-affirming."*

—Luciano Pavarotti, opera singer

❧

$\mathcal{S}$URROUNDED BY FARMS, the tiny village of Roncole is situated in the
northern province of Parma in Italy. Located about 65 miles southeast of the
bustling city of Milan, it is guarded by the Apennine Mountains on the south and west
and the rushing waters of the River Po to the north. Nestled in the flat, fertile Po Valley,
three miles from the market town of Busseto, the village has been renamed Roncole
Verdi in honor of its most famous resident, who was born there on October 9, 1813. The
next day the infant was baptized in the parish church of Saint Michael the Archangel.
He was given the name Giuseppe Fortunio Francesco, but the birth registrar recorded
his name using the French version of Joseph Fortunin François.

Shutterstock

Giuseppe's parents had married in 1805. His family lived in the village inn, which sat on a crossroads in the middle of Roncole. The modest building also contained a general store. His father, Carlo, was the innkeeper who ran the tavern and oversaw the grocery store. The tavern and grocery were separated from the rooms the family occupied on the first and second floors of the house.

While most of the people in the village were illiterate, Carlo could read and write as well as keep accounting records. Luigia Uttini, Giuseppe's gentle and pretty mother, came from a family that had settled in the medieval town of Piacenza on the banks of the River Po. Her father was also an innkeeper; after her marriage she helped in the grocery store and earned some extra money by selling the yarn

The house where Giuseppe Verdi was born in the small village of Roncole, Italy.

DIVIDED ITALY

The Romans once ruled a united Italy, giving the people who lived there unity and a common culture. When the Roman Empire collapsed in 476, several Germanic tribes invaded and conquered the land, separating Italy into three regions. Their domination ended in 774 when they were defeated by Charlemagne.

In 962 the king of Germany, Otto the Great, was proclaimed the next Roman emperor and the Holy Roman Empire was established. Over the centuries the popes and various rulers sought to control a patchwork of independent city-states, called communes. Except for Rome, which was controlled by the Vatican, the residents of these city-states were governed by local nobles or high-ranking members of the clergy. Self-governing communes arose, allowing the influential residents of each community a small voice against the power of those who ruled them. The major city-states were located in Milan, Genoa, Venice, Florence, and Pisa. From 1805 to 1814 the entire peninsula was united under Napoleon, but when he was defeated the country was once again divided. A social and political movement known as *il Risorgimento* (the Resurgence) led to the reunification of the country in 1861.

that she spun. The couple had been married for eight years before their first child was born. His birth was a cause for celebration and a source of joy for the family.

A baby girl, Giuseppa Francesca, was born three years after Giuseppe. She liked to follow him around. Her brother was a shy and quiet child, slender with grey eyes and thick brown hair. He did not like the loud, rough play of the other boys in his village. Giuseppe would not join in their wrestling matches or hoop rolling games.

During the first few years of Giuseppe's childhood life in Italy was difficult because a war was being fought. When Giuseppe was born the country of Italy did not exist. The land was divided into several small states, each one under the domination of a foreign power. Each state had its own dialect of the Italian language and its own paper money and coins. Passports were required to travel from one state to another.

In 1796 the French army, under the command of Napoleon Bonaparte, had invaded and gained control of northern Italy from Milan to Venice. The same year Verdi's parents married, Napoleon had been crowned as the king of Italy. Within a few years the French took over the entire peninsula. (That is why the record of Verdi's birth was written in French instead of Italian.)

Play Hoop Rolling

HOOP ROLLING, sometimes called hoop bowling or trundling, was recommended for good health by the ancient Greek physician Hippocrates. For centuries it was a popular pastime for both boys and girls throughout the world. It gave children a chance to go outdoors, where they could play either alone or with a group, rolling their hoops along the ground with the help of a sticklike tool. Hula hoops are modern versions of this very old game.

You'll Need
∞ 1 or more hoops, such as hula hoops or bicycle rims (the hoops may be made of wood, metal, or plastic)
∞ 1 or more 12-inch-long wooden dowels
∞ 1 or more players

Practice rolling your hoop on a flat, slightly declining surface. Use the dowel to prod the hoop along. It will take some practice to learn how to control your hoop.

If you are playing alone, you can try to pass the hoop through two objects placed about a foot apart. Narrow the opening between the objects when you get good at rolling the hoop through them. Another game to try is to roll the hoop down a twisted path.

With a group you can roll the hoops into one another to knock down your opponent's hoops or race your hoops against one another.

An engraving of Napoleon Bonaparte from Harper's Monthly, 1879. Shutterstock

French soldiers were stationed throughout the land while battles raged between them and their foes. The story was often told in Roncole that in 1814, during one of these battles, a frightened Luigia ran to the nearby church to find sanctuary (safety). When the soldiers barged into the church Luigia managed to scramble up the steep steps into the bell tower and hide with her young son. From this time forward, young Giuseppe's life would be intertwined with the Italian people's struggle to gain control of their own country.

But even war on their own soil could not intrude on Italian culture; the people retained their religion, language, and customs. For the residents of Roncole life revolved around hard work, family, the Catholic church, good food, and great music.

ITALIAN FOODS

Italians are proud that the world's oldest cookbook still in existence, *De re coquinaria* (On Cookery), is attributed to a fellow countryman who relished good food—the first-century Roman Marcus Gavius Apicius. The cookbook presents a collection of almost 500 recipes for various dishes.

Certain foods are associated with Italy. There are differences throughout the country in Italians' choice of ingredients and cooking style, but the basic foods used to prepare many Italian dishes are the same. The Italian peninsula is separated from the rest of the European continent by a high mountain range named the Alps. Because mountains also divide the Italian peninsula, each region developed its own recipes based on its climate and the fertility of the soil. Many regional foods were influenced by who ruled in the past; the Greeks, the French, North Africans, and the Austrians all left their stamp on Italian cuisine.

Italians enjoy pasta, but in the northern parts of the coun-

An illustration from an early edition of De re coquinaria, *the world's oldest cookbook.* Courtesy of the Richard L. D. & Marjorie J. Morse Department of Special Collections, Kansas State University

try people prefer their pasta to be fresh and soft while the people living in the southern region developed dry pasta. The residents of the southern city of Naples like spicy foods and enjoy seafood and olive oil in their recipes, but those living in northern Bologna favor less spicy recipes and prefer to use butter and meat. In the past, the southern region was poorer and more isolated so the people had to be inventive with ingredients available locally; it is believed that is why they invented pizza.

Off to School

GIUSEPPE BEGAN attending a school run by the local priests when he was four. The priests taught their students how to read and write, plus some Italian grammar, arithmetic, and catechism (the basic principles of the Catholic religion).

One of Giuseppe's first teachers, Don Biastrocchi, was not a clergyman but the organist at the church of Saint Michael the Archangel. The organist accompanied the congregation during their singing of hymns. Biastrocchi was the first person to recognize that the youngster had musical talent and offered to give him lessons on the church organ. He also told Giuseppe's parents that their son had a great gift.

In 1820, when Giuseppe was seven, his parents were able to buy him a broken-down spinet (a harpsichord with strings that were plucked by points of leather on the ends of leather hammers). These old-fashioned and outdated instruments had been replaced by the more modern piano, but even a harpsichord was an unusual acquisition for a family with a limited income in the 19th century. People who came to Carlo and Luigia's tavern remarked that their son must be extremely talented for them to make such an extravagant purchase.

Carlo asked Stefano Cavaletti, a harpsichord maker, to repair the instrument. Cavaletti fixed the broken hammers and any other worn-out

Make Your Own Pasta

❖

PASTA IS an important part of the Italian diet. It is made out of flour, eggs, and water blended and fashioned into many different shapes and sizes. Homemade pasta always tastes better than store-bought pasta. Try this simple pasta recipe at home.

Adult supervision required.

You'll Need
- Large bowl
- Wooden spoon
- 2 cups flour (plus additional for kneading)
- 1 teaspoon salt
- 3 large eggs
- 1 teaspoon water
- 1 teaspoon olive oil
- Medium bowl
- Fork
- Knife
- Plastic wrap
- Rolling pin
- Large pot
- Strainer

Place the flour in the large bowl and mix in the salt. Make a well in the center to pour in the other ingredients.

In the medium bowl beat the remaining ingredients (eggs, water, and olive oil) with the fork and pour the mixture into the well. Using your hands, work the ingredients together until they form a ball of dough. Remove the dough from the bowl and place on a lightly floured surface. Continue kneading the dough until it is not sticky and looks smooth.

Divide the dough into four pieces with the knife; cover three of them with plastic wrap. Keep a light layer of flour on the other piece of dough so it does not stick on the rolling pin and roll out the dough to about 1/8 inch thick. Fold and roll out the dough a few more times, getting it thin enough for you to see your hand through it. Let the rolled out batch rest for about a half hour before cutting it with the knife into 2-inch-wide strips and then into 1-inch-long pieces. Repeat these steps for each piece of dough.

Fill the large pot with water and heat it to boiling. Add the pasta and let it simmer for three to four minutes. Have an adult pour it into a strainer to drain. Serve it with your favorite sauce. *Buon Appetito!*

parts. After he made the repairs Cavaletti wrote a note, which he left hidden inside the spinet, stating that he had repaired it free of charge because of "the good disposition of the boy Giuseppe Verdi for learning to play the instrument, which is itself reward enough for me for my trouble." Giuseppe understood this gift represented sacrifice and love from his parents. He treasured the instrument and kept it for the rest of his life.

Young Giuseppe progressed so quickly that after a year of lessotns the organist announced that he was finished teaching the child. Biastrocchi was an older man who was ready to

A piano built in 1803.

TYPES OF PIANOS

Pianos are built in a variety of shapes and styles. There are two categories that describe these types: vertical, or upright, and horizontal, or grand. The types reflect the needs of the player and the available space for the instrument.

Upright pianos have their strings placed vertically and are all 58 inches in width. Spinets take up the least amount of space and are about three feet tall. The console piano ranges from 40 to 43 inches high. The studio piano, usually found in music schools, contains a larger sounding board and longer strings; it can be four feet high. A full-size or professional piano is from four to five feet tall.

Grand pianos have their strings housed horizontally; they are measured from the front of the keyboard to the farthest point at the back of the piano. These instruments are used by professional musicians in **solo** performances or in concert. Grand pianos range in size. A petite grand is about four and one-half feet in length; a baby grand is about five and one-half feet long. Medium and parlor styles stretch from five and one-half feet to just over six feet. A professional grand or ballroom grand ranges from six and one-half to seven and one-half feet. The concert grand can be over nine feet in length.

retire; he had the boy play the organ during church services fairly often. Two years later, when Giuseppe was 10 years old, his teacher passed away. The boy was asked to continue as the organist in the place of worship in which he had been baptized. He also sang in the choir and served as an altar boy (an assistant to the clergy) in this church.

One time Giuseppe was not paying attention during a church service. The priest tried to get the young altar boy's attention, the story goes, but he did not seem to notice. This made the priest so angry he walked over to the boy and kicked him hard. Giuseppe tumbled down the steps, striking his head before he passed out unconscious on the floor of the church. After regaining his awareness, Giuseppe looked at the priest and said, "May God strike you down." In 1828, a number of years later, lightning hit another nearby church in which this priest was officiating. The lightning strike actually killed the priest along with several members of the congregation who were attending the service. Superstitious local residents repeated the story of "Verdi's Curse" for many years.

On to Busseto

BECAUSE THEIR son was an attentive and hard-working student, Giuseppe's parents wanted him to continue his education. There were no opportunities for that in their village, so Carlo and Luigia made the decision to send their son away. He would not have to go too far, however. In 1823 Giuseppe left Roncole and moved to Busseto to attend a *ginnasio* (secondary school). The larger town of Busseto could offer him much more.

Since Giuseppe could not walk the three miles back to his home every day, his fam-

This Italian advertisement imagines Verdi as a boy, enraptured by a violinist playing in his village.

ily arranged for him to live in the home of a family friend, a cobbler whom everyone called Pugnatta. The cobbler charged only 30 *centesimi* (about 3 cents) for each day that he provided a place to sleep and food for the boy. On Sundays and holidays Giuseppe would hike back to Roncole to see his family and play the organ at Saint Michael the Archangel. Many people noticed that in good weather the boy made the trip barefoot to spare his shoes. Another often-told anecdote from Verdi's childhood recounts how one Sunday evening the extremely tired youngster fell into a water-filled ditch as he was returning to Busseto. Luckily, an elderly woman heard his cries and pulled him out.

A prominent resident of Busseto, Antonio Barezzi was a well-to-do owner of a distillery (a place where liquor is manufactured). In addition he was a wholesale grocer from whom Giuseppe's father, Carlo, bought supplies for his home and business. For years Carlo had walked from Roncole to Busseto once a week to pick up his order of supplies. The men had many conversations and knew each other well. Barezzi was an amateur musician who played several instruments including the flute and the violin. He also was the founder and president of the local amateur **orchestra**, the Busseto Philharmonic Society.

Music in 19th-century Italy revolved around the opera house, the town orchestra and band,

the music school, and church music. Many inhabitants of each town who considered themselves to be amateur musicians taught music, played church instruments, and sang in the choir. Some also were involved in the band or orchestra that performed at concerts and events. Local orchestras were often allotted funds by the municipalities to supplement the money they received from patrons or earned through ticket sales or private performances. As opera was extremely popular with the Italian public, opera houses had been erected in almost every large city in Italy. Most small towns could not afford to build an opera house but they often had their own opera society.

Busseto did not have a theater or an opera house, so the rehearsals and performances of the Busseto Philharmonic Society took place in a spacious room in Barezzi's large house. The members of this orchestra performed several concerts each year and provided the musicians for public events. Many residents of Busseto had a family member in the orchestra. Barezzi was well liked among the people of this town for his support and leadership role.

The composer Ferdinando Provesi was a friend of Barezzi's. Provesi was the music director of the Busseto Philharmonic Society and director of the municipal music school. He was also the organist at the cathedral of San Bartolomeo. Barezzi asked Provesi to

Verdi's early patron Antonio Barezzi.

teach his protégé, and after hearing the boy perform, Provesi offered to provide these lessons free of charge. Giuseppe started his lessons in music composition and harmony with a man who was considered to be a master of counterpoint.

Provesi was an excellent teacher. He had Giuseppe compose church music, marches, and many types of instrumental music. The young composer wrote hundreds of pieces during this time; unfortunately, he did not keep most of them. Looking back on those days Verdi summed up:

> *From the ages of thirteen to eighteen I wrote a mixed assortment of pieces: marches for the band by the hundred, perhaps as many sinfonie [symphonies] that were used in church, in the theater and at concerts, five or six concertos and sets of variations for pianoforte, which I played myself at concerts, many serenades, cantatas (arias, duets and many trios), and various pieces of church music, of which I only remember a Stabat mater [a Latin hymn].*

At the age of 13 Giuseppe gave his first concert on the school organ. One year later he was composing for Busseto Philharmonic Society concerts. When he was 16 he applied for a position as the organist at a church in another town not far from Busseto but did not get the job.

Music Note: WHAT IS COUNTERPOINT?

The word "counterpoint" comes from the Latin *punctus contra punctum* meaning "point against point" or "note against note." It is a technique composers use to combine two or more independent melodic lines in a way that creates a harmonic relationship. Each melodic line is called a voice.

A theme or subject is introduced by the first voice then copied by another; this is called imitation. While the imitative voice repeats the subject, the first voice goes on to a new subject called the counter-subject. Other voices may be added. When we sing a round like the one in the song "Oh, How Lovely Is the Evening," we are performing simple counterpoint. (Note: the * marks the place where the next voice enters.)

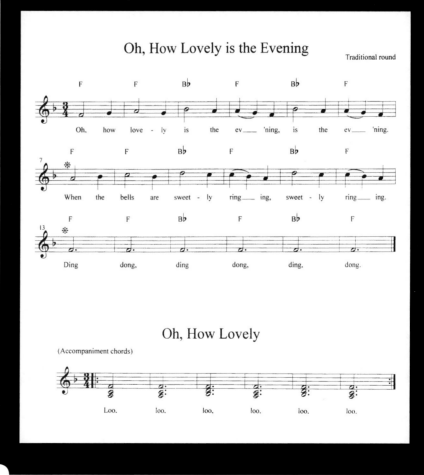

9

In 1828, when his student graduated from the ginnasio, Provesi offered him a position in his music school. Giuseppe remained in Busseto continuing his music lessons and teaching for three more years. When Provesi was unwell

his student took over his duties for the church. Verdi was also writing pieces for the Busseto orchestra, which performed them almost as soon as the ink was dry. The residents who attended these concerts praised his works.

When Giuseppe was 17, Antonio Barezzi became a true patron to the young composer, taking him into his home and family while supplying the funds that allowed him to pursue his education. Giuseppe was treated as one of the members of the household. With four daughters and two sons of their own, Barezzi and his wife, Maria, offered more than room and board to the young man. Giuseppe's best friend, Giovanni, was one of their sons. Their lively, auburn-haired daughter Margherita, seven months younger than Giuseppe, would also become an important person in his life. The newest member of the household gave Margherita piano and voice lessons. A few years later, as they got to know each other, the young couple fell in love.

A Stroke of Luck

TWO YEARS later, Provesi announced that he had finished teaching young Verdi; he further advised that it was time for him to attend a music conservatory or a university. Giuseppe knew that his parents could not afford to pay for these

---

Compose Rap Counterpoint

THE FINALE (last musical number of the **act** or opera) in Verdi's opera *Falstaff* is a wonderful example of counterpoint. It is a complex model, but counterpoint does not have to be elaborate. You can write something simpler.

You'll Need

∞ A CD or MP3 download of "Tutto nel mondo è burla . . . Tutti gabbati!" (Everything in the world is a jest) from *Falstaff*

∞ A music-listening device (such as an iPod, computer, or CD player) or a computer with Internet access to YouTube

∞ 2 or more people

∞ Tape recorder (if you want to tape your rap counterpoint)

Listen to the final fugue (see sidebar on page 16) in the opera *Falstaff*, "Tutto nel mondo è burla . . . Tutti gabbati!" (Everything in the world is a jest). Notice how the voices begin at different times and how they imitate each other, overlap, and work together.

Write a brief sentence that will be the theme or subject of your rap counterpoint. An example would be "I love summer vacation." Add a second voice (or more) to repeat the subject. Decide when the voices should alternate and when they should overlap each other. Lastly, determine how you want to end the composition; for example, "Why does summer have to end?" Rehearse it a few times before you record it.

expensive institutions. He was disheartened by the prospect that he would have to return to Roncole and work in his father's tavern.

Barezzi searched for a way to allow Giuseppe to continue his music education. Perhaps the patron could find a scholarship or some type of employment that would let the young man earn enough to support himself and study at the same time. Meanwhile, Barezzi urged his protégé to remain in Busseto until this problem could be worked out.

The Busseto Philharmonic Society arranged a concert of Verdi's music. All the important people in the city were invited to attend. His teacher and his patron were thrilled by the opportunity to sit in the audience and listen to the beautiful music. Everyone agreed that this young composer had terrific talent. Giuseppe was equally pleased by the response to his music. He was sorry to be leaving Busseto but looking forward to the future.

Giuseppe's father presented an application to the Monte di Pietà, a local charity, requesting funds for a scholarship to pay for Verdi to attend the Milan Conservatory of Music. In February 1832 the charity granted the request and said that a scholarship of 300 lire would be available the following year. Filled with

PATRONS AND THE ARTS

The word "patron" comes from the Latin word for father; it means benefactor or someone who supports someone else. From the 14th through the 18th centuries the patronage system was an institution in Europe. Patrons were wealthy people, usually members of the nobility or clergy, who could afford to finance artists' and musicians' lives while the artists created art or music. The influential men and women paid for these works either for their private use or to entertain their guests. Sometimes a patron hired an artist to produce work for a church. Their money and encouragement allowed many masterpieces to be created.

Financially supporting artists and having input into what they produced enhanced the social standing of a patron. Patrons were seen as prominent members of society; their prestige grew if they could be the benefactor of several artists. The recipients of this support were not always happy with the situation since they were often told exactly what they had to create. Artists had to be careful not to anger their patrons as they were their sole source of income under this system.

delight, Carlo wrote to thank the officer of the charity who had sent this good news.

Since this scholarship money would not be accessible until 1833, Barezzi promised to advance Giuseppe the funds that would be needed for his first year of study. What luck! The hopeful student packed his belongings and traveled to Milan to take the audition required for admission to the conservatory. ❧

TURNING DISAPPOINTMENT INTO SUCCESS

1832–1840

"I adore art ... when I am alone with my notes,

my heart pounds and the tears stream from my eyes,

and my emotion and my joys are too much to bear."

—Giuseppe Verdi

VERDI ARRIVED IN Milan in June 1832. Milan was the capital of the Austrian-ruled province of Lombardy-Venice and the cultural center of northern Italy. Before he could audition for a spot as a student at the conservatory, Verdi had to fill out an application and hand in some of his compositions for the entrance committee to examine. These included a fugue that they had required he compose using a subject they provided. At his audition he had to play the piano to demonstrate his musical talent. Finally, the forms completed and the audition over, Verdi anxiously waited for a response from the conservatory.

When no letter arrived from the school, Verdi started to worry. He decided to go and talk to Alessandro Rolla, one of the professors at the conservatory who had been on the entrance committee. Provesi had provided him with a letter of introduction that he was to give to this violin professor. The professor gave Verdi the awful news that his application had been turned down. He further counseled the young man to give up his plan to attend the

Music Note: WHAT IS A FUGUE?

The word "fugue" comes from the Latin word *fuga*, which means flight. In a fugue the short melodies, called subjects, fly from one voice to the other. The basis of a fugue is counterpoint. A fugue may be composed for instruments or singers; the lines are called voices even if an instrument is presenting the piece.

The subject is the unifying theme and focal point of the music. It is stated first in one voice and then imitated in another; this is called the answer. While the second voice is added, the first voice continues with a countersubject. The subject appears again in a third voice while the first two voices create a contrasting texture against the third voice. Once the voices have presented the theme, the first part of the fugue, the exposition, is complete. A fugue alternates between the exposition sections and interludes called episodes. As the work unfolds, the tension builds as the subject is presented in a different manner, such as being played in another key (the pitch that serves as the tonal center of the music).

Many fugues were composed during the Baroque era (1600 to 1750). One of the most famous composers of this time was Johann Sebastian Bach, who wrote *The Art of the Fugue*, which depicts many ways to compose in this form. The fugue style of composition was not popular after the Baroque era ended, but it is still an enjoyable form of music to hear.

This unfinished fugue, "Die Kunst der Fuge" (The Art of the Fugue) by Johann Sebastian Bach, was published in 1751, one year after his death. International Music Score Library Project (IMSLP)

school and instead to look for a private teacher. Verdi was devastated by the news.

Later Verdi learned more details of this decision. First of all, the officials at the school had believed that, at 19, Verdi was too old; other students entering the conservatory were usually younger. Their second reason was that since he was not from the Lombardy area where the school was located, they viewed him as a foreigner and therefore refused him entrance to their conservatory. The committee had a rule that students from other states could not attend and saw no reason to change it for this young man. Lastly, one of the piano teachers had not liked the way he held his hands while performing on the instrument; therefore, the committee had found that his piano technique was unorthodox.

The reasons given for this rejection struck the young man like sharp needles piercing his heart. He kept the rejection letter for the rest of his days; it was a painful reminder of a dreadful time in his life.

An Alternate Path

VERDI KNEW that he had to inform his family, his patron, and his former teacher about his rejection. Barezzi, always seeking solutions, agreed with the professor's suggestion.

Perceptively Listen to a Composition

— ❀ —

TO UNDERSTAND how a composition works and why a composer wrote a piece of music a certain way, you need to perceptively listen to the piece and answer questions about it. Perceptive listening to music is an art.

You'll Need

∞ A CD or MP3 download of "The Triumphal March" from *Aida*, act 2, scene 2

∞ A music-listening device (such as an iPod, computer, or CD player) or a computer with Internet access to watch "The Triumphal March" on YouTube

∞ Pen and paper or a word processing program

"The Triumphal March" is the finale of act 2 of the opera *Aida* that Verdi composed in 1869. The opera is set in ancient Egypt. In this **scene** the Egyptian general Radames and his troops march in front of the Egyptian pharaoh and nobility where they receive a hero's welcome for their triumph over the Ethiopians.

The first time you listen to "The Triumphal March" just enjoy the music. Next, listen to the piece several times while looking for answers to the questions below. It takes many listening sessions to be able to thoroughly understand a great composition. Jot down your answers while you listen and share your thoughts with your music teacher or write a report for your class in school. What do you imagine when hearing the music?

1. Which instrument opens the work?
2. Why do you think Verdi started the march this way?
3. What is the rhythm? How would you walk to the music?
4. What changes do you hear after the opening of the work?
5. What does the chorus add to the work?
6. What is the mood of the song the chorus sings?
7. Can you tell by the changes in the music where a ballet begins?
8. How does the work end?

He would pay for private music lessons. They found a teacher who had wonderful credentials: the composer and concertmaster (first violinist and leader of the orchestra) Vincenzo Lavigna was available and willing to teach Verdi. He had looked at Verdi's compositions and found it strange that the conservatory had turned down such a promising musician.

Barezzi was aware that this new arrangement would be more costly. Besides room and board, his protégé would need a piano and music **scores** for practice and music composition paper. It was determined that Giuseppe Seletti, a friend of Barezzi, was willing to house the young man while he studied with Lavigna. But living in someone's home in the midst of

MUSIC CONSERVATORIES

Music conservatories are high-level, specialized schools that teach and conduct research about music. Good music conservatory programs are accredited; this means they have met the standards required by an agency appointed to determine the quality and value of the available courses. Generally students attend these schools for a degree.

These institutions offer courses in music history, theory, composition, performance, and conducting and provide training for voice or instruments. Faculty members are drawn from experienced, professional musicians who might still be working in the music field. Often the faculty is enhanced by famous musicians or composers who come to the school for a semester or longer. Guest artists invited to the school expose the students to some of the world's best musicians. Conservatories provide opportunities for their students to perform as soloists or participate as members of an orchestra, choir, or **ensemble** (a group of performers).

The Milan Conservatory was founded by a royal decree from Napoleon in 1807 and opened the following year. Even though it did not accept Verdi as a student, the conservatory named the college the Giuseppe Verdi Conservatory after his death. Today this prestigious institution is Italy's largest music school and is a part of the Italian university system.

Milan's society meant Verdi would require some formal clothes—he could not dress in the more casual and careless manner of students.

With composition lessons arranged, the composer could enjoy the sights of a city much larger than Busseto. Milan had more than 150,000 residents in 1832 and offered many attractions. It housed works of art from the painter and sculptor Michelangelo and the genius Leonardo da Vinci. The builders of Sforza Castle had started construction in the 14th century. Some of the ceilings in the castle had been painted by da Vinci during the Renaissance. When Verdi arrived in Milan the Sforza Castle was undergoing renovations.

The city also boasted some old and magnificent architecture in its churches. The medieval church called Basilica di Sant'Ambrogio (the Cathedral of Saint Ambrose) was built between the years 379 and 386. Named for Milan's patron saint, it had originally been built outside of the old walled city, which had, over the centuries, grown to surround it.

Another magnificent sight was the amazing spires and stained glass windows of the Gothic cathedral the Duomo di Milano (the Milan Cathedral), which had taken almost six centuries to complete. One of the largest churches in the world, it is topped by a 357-foot-tall spire designed by Francesco Croce that is in turn topped by a gilded copper statue called *The*

The great Duomo di Milano (Milan Cathedral) is the fourth-largest church in the world.

Madonnina, carved by Giuseppe Perego. The stained glass windows are glorious works of art.

Lessons with Lavigna began. The teacher sent glowing reports to the Monte di Pietà, the

A stained glass window in the Duomo di Milano.
Shutterstock

charity in Busseto, making them aware that he believed that their money was well spent. Lavigna was certain that Verdi was gaining information and enjoying his teaching. Apparently, however, Verdi had a totally different image of these lessons. Years later, Verdi wrote a letter recalling his experiences as a student in Milan. "Lavigna was very strong on counterpoint," he wrote. But, "In the three years spent with him I did nothing but canons and fugues, fugues and canons of every kind. Nobody taught me **orchestration** or how to treat dramatic music." And yet, Verdi was grateful that Lavigna was a good teacher; he concluded this letter saying, "He was learned and I wish all teachers were like him."

Musical Milan

LAVIGNA ENCOURAGED his student to attend the theater and the opera. Verdi's patron Barezzi had to buy a subscription to the Milan opera house for Verdi. La Scala, Milan's opera house, had opened in 1778; all of Milan gathered there to attend the latest work—if they could afford to buy a ticket.

Lavigna suggested that his student attend a rehearsal of the Milan Philharmonic Society featuring Joseph Haydn's oratorio *The Creation*. Pietro Massini, the director of this orchestra,

had met Verdi at Lavigna's home. When the assistant **conductors** did not arrive on time, Massini asked Verdi to play the bass accompaniment on the piano. Verdi began to accompany the rehearsing singers; soon he was playing the music with his left hand while conducting with his right. Massini was so impressed with his abilities that he asked Verdi to take part in the performance.

Verdi was happy to take part in the musical life of Milan, even though he was not paid for his efforts. He was hopeful that his association with important musicians like Massini would lead to being commissioned to compose an opera. Massini became a helpful supporter and put the hopeful young man in touch with a few librettists who might write the texts to his future operas.

Growing Up and Moving On

FERDINANDO PROVESI, Verdi's previous teacher back in Busseto, had died. This unfortunate death caused a dispute between two factions in the small town. The now-vacant position of music director had to be filled. Barezzi and his friends wanted to wait until Verdi completed his studies in Milan so that he could return to Busseto and take over his former teacher's post. This faction also expected

Make a "Stained Glass Window"

DURING THE 13th and 14th centuries in Italy huge churches were constructed with thick walls and small windows that did not let in much light. To illuminate and beautify the cathedrals, artisans created magnificent stained glass windows. Verdi would have seen many such windows while walking around Milan. Like a stained glass window, a sun catcher uses light to brighten up and decorate a space. It is a colorful addition to any room.

You'll Need

∞ Old towel or newspapers
∞ Sketch paper
∞ Pencil
∞ Ruler
∞ Permanent black marker
∞ Crayons or colored pencils
∞ 10- by 12-inch piece of clear acrylic
∞ Gel paint in various colors
∞ Paintbrush
∞ 1 cup water
∞ Paper towels
∞ Hole punch
∞ 4 inches string or yarn

1. Cover your work surface with the old towel or newspapers. Measure and draw a 10-inch by 12-inch rectangle on your sketch paper. In pencil, sketch a picture to fit inside this rectangle. You might choose flowers or an abstract arrangement of shapes such as triangles, circles, and so on as your subject.

2. Divide the picture into several different shapes, outlining them in pencil. Trace over the outlines of the shapes with the black marker. Color inside the outlines with crayons or colored pencils.

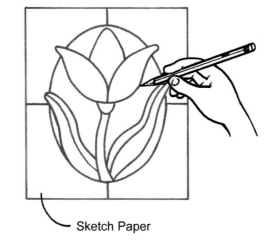

Sketch Paper

3. Place the acrylic on top of your paper pattern and copy the outline of the shapes onto the acrylic with the black marker.

4. Use the brush to apply the paint to the acrylic inside the outlines, following the color palette you developed on your sketch paper. Clean the brush in the water when you are finished using a color.

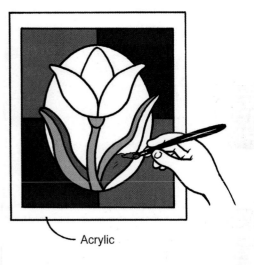

Acrylic

5. Let the paint dry. Check to see if there are any shapes that may need another coat of paint. Apply another coat to those shapes. Let the paint dry and then reapply black marker to the outlines.

6. When everything is dry, punch a hole in the middle of the acrylic ½ inch down from the top. Attach and tie the string to hang the sun catcher in a window.

that the applicants for the organist position would be judged through a competition that was normally held to determine which of the candidates was best suited. On June 20, 1834, Verdi arrived in Busseto expecting to take part in the contest.

The faction headed by Barezzi was shocked to learn that a rival group had already appointed Giovanni Ferrari as the organist for the church of San Bartolomeo—without any competition. Barezzi and his friends were enraged by this brazen appointment. Verdi's supporters asked the government officials to require a competition. While they were waiting for an answer from the authorities in Parma, it was decided that the Busseto philharmonic members would

LA SCALA

In 1776 a fire destroyed the old theater in Milan. Empress Maria Theresa of Austria, the country ruling Milan, approved the architectural plans for a theater designed by the Italian architect Giuseppe Piermarini, but she required the people who bought the expensive and exclusive private box seats to provide the funds to cover the cost of building a new home for opera in the city.

The theater was constructed on land that had been the site of the Gothic church of Santa Maria alla Scala, built in 1381. The Nuovo Regio Ducale Teatro alla Scala (the New Royal-Ducal Theatre at La Scala) opened on August 3, 1778. Everyone soon short-ened the name to La Scala, which means "the staircase" or "ladder."

The theater could accommodate an audience of almost 3,000. The main floor did not contain chairs, so the poorer attendees stood during the performances. The wealthy patrons of the house purchased box seats for the season. The boxes were layered on top of one another upon the walls, and patrons spent a great deal of money trying to outshine one another in the decoration of these fancy boxes. There was no orchestra pit in the theater. The first work presented at La Scala was Antonio Salieri's *L'Europa Riconosciuta* (Europa Revealed).

La Scala Opera House in Milan, Italy.

no longer perform at church services. Six months later, some people were still so angry that they got into a fistfight in the church on Christmas.

Old rivalries, rumors, and misinformation were the causes that led to this feud between the residents of Busseto. Verdi was now unofficially engaged to Antonio Barezzi's daughter Margherita. She had made statements that led many townspeople to believe that Verdi was very busy composing an opera in Milan and probably would not consider returning to their village for the position. The factions were still inflamed when in 1835 a response finally came from the authorities in Parma. The government officials decided that the positions of organist

Music Note: WHAT IS AN ORATORIO?

An oratorio is a musical genre closely related to opera. The name comes from an oratory or prayer hall, the place where these works were first performed. These large-scale concert works are usually based on sacred or religious subjects; many of the stories portrayed in an oratorio are taken from the Bible.

Like an opera, an oratorio is sung with an orchestra but without the costumes, scenery, and dramatic acting found in the opera house. The chorus has a larger role in this type of work and a narrator often introduces the scenes and the characters.

The first oratorio was composed in the 16th century by the Italian Emilio de'Cavalieri. His *Rappresentatione di anima e di corpo* (*The Representation of the Soul and the Body*) is a three-act work that debuted in Rome in 1600. During the 17th century the oratorio captured the imagination of German composers like Johann Sebastian Bach and George Frideric Handel. The best-known piece in this genre is Handel's *Messiah*; the magnificent music of this oratorio is performed frequently.

Sketch of an oratorio rehearsal, 1869. Library of Congress LC-USZ62-95677

and music director of the philharmonic would be divided into two jobs. The position of music director would be the only one decided by a competition, and Giovanni Ferrari would continue as the organist.

Verdi had gone back to Milan to finish his studies with Lavigna. The 23-year-old then returned to Busseto in time for the competition, which was held in February 1836. Verdi won the contest and was appointed the music director of the Busseto philharmonic in March. The organist-position episode had made Verdi unhappy; he was particularly angry with the people, including the priests, who had hired Ferrari without giving Verdi a chance. The salary for the divided position that he had been offered as the town music master was quite small. He was to sign a nine-year contract that had to be renewed every three years.

Four days before Verdi signed the contract for the position, he became formally engaged to Margherita. They were married on May 4 and took a brief honeymoon to Milan. They settled into an apartment in Busseto paid for by Verdi's father-in-law. In the next three years Verdi composed for and directed the Busseto Philharmonic Society and gave private music lessons. The couple quickly had two children.

Music Note: WHAT IS A CANTATA?

The word "cantata" comes from the Italian word *cantare,* which means to sing. A cantata is a large-scale vocal work; it can be religious or secular. The genre originated in Italy during the 17th century. A cantata is divided into several movements of **arias** (elaborate songs for one voice), solos, **duets, recitatives** (passages of text that are a combination of speaking and singing), and choruses that are accompanied by orchestral instruments.

Johann Sebastian Bach was a prolific cantata composer; he wrote over 200 of these works for religious and secular occasions. When he wrote music for German Lutheran churches he had to compose a new cantata for each Sunday and holiday. Lutherans often chose this musical genre for their church services; cantatas became an important part of their sacred music.

Their daughter, Virginia, was born in 1837 followed a year later by the birth of their son, Icilio Romano.

Verdi was pleased that he was able to provide a living for his growing family through his music. He was always searching for ways to satisfy the public with his compositions and to expand his options. Realizing the Italian love for opera matched his own feelings about the genre, he became determined to concentrate on writing operas. This was the way he would assure the comfort of the family he adored.

When the three-year renewal period on Verdi's contract was over, he decided to leave Busseto. In a letter to the mayor of Busseto he wrote that he was saddened by feeling that he had not been more useful in "this most unhappy town of mine."

Having decided that he wanted to compose opera, Verdi understood that his goal could not be realized in any small town. He needed to move back to Milan. In 1836 he had signed a contract with a Milanese music society and composed a **cantata** for them honoring the Austrian emperor Ferdinand I.

In 1836 Verdi had also composed *Rocester*, an opera that he hoped to have performed in a theater in Parma. This plan did not work out. However, Verdi had also sent the manuscript to Massini in Milan. His friend showed it to Bartolomeo Merelli, the **impresario** (director) of

Solve an Opera Word Search

IN ORDER to understand operatic terminology you will need to learn the vocabulary used to discuss opera. Many of the words about opera come from Italian, German, or French languages because many of the early composers came from the countries in which those languages were spoken.

If you are using a library book, copy the word search onto paper first.

You'll Need
∞ Pen or pencil
∞ Copy of this page

Find and circle the words:

```
d t a i i t e u d i t e
l e e a e l n c o a m l
o m s a a m l h n r a s
o p s n r s d o d u s c
n o i s s i m r e t n i
a f f a v r a u b a e m
r d b a r r r s u r n a
p o c o n d u c t o r n
o o n e n s e m b l e y
s e l i b r e t t o o d
t e l o i r t b n c t u
c r n t s o r n l l t s
```

aria
bass
chorus
coloratura
conductor
debut
diva
duet
dynamics
ensemble
finale
intermission
libretto
solo
soprano
tempo
trio
tenor

La Scala. Always seeking new works to present, Merelli was interested. The debut was scheduled for the 1839 Carnival season (springtime), but one of the main singers became ill and the opening was postponed.

Merelli rescheduled the premiere for the autumn, but first he suggested that some changes should be made to the work. During the delay Verdi revised the opera and renamed it *Oberto, conte di San Bonifacio* (Oberto, Count of Saint Boniface) a two-act work with a modified **libretto** (written text or script) by the poet and novelist Temistocle Solera. Verdi was pleased that the impresario of La Scala had given him this opportunity even though he was an unknown composer. In October Verdi resigned his post in Busseto and in February 1839 Verdi and his family moved to Milan.

As the impresario had promised, *Oberto, conte di San Bonifacio* debuted on November 17, 1839. It was well received by the audiences and critics attending Milan's first-rate theater. Merelli was also pleased with the reception of the new opera and extended its number of performances. He offered the composer a contract for three new works to be debuted during the next two years. The music publisher Giovanni Ricordi bought the score of the opera to sell to the public and paid Verdi handsomely for the privilege.

Verdi's life was on track as a composer; he was very happy. Next Merelli requested that he compose an **opera buffa (comic opera)** since he was lacking a comic work for the next season's **repertory**. Verdi had a choice of several librettos; he selected one that had been written in 1818. The older libretto was renamed *Un giorno di regno* (A One-Day Reign, or King for a Day) and Verdi began composing the score. He was experiencing a sore throat while he worked, but that was not going to change his cheerful mood.

Tragedy Strikes

VERDI'S JOYFUL life as a successful composer was interrupted by tragedy. Mortality rates were high during the early and mid-19th century. Unsanitary conditions caused the spread of illnesses. Houses were damp and cleaning equipment was primitive. Indoor bathrooms did not exist, and personal hygiene was poor. Water, usually pumped from wells, was unfiltered and could easily be contaminated. Streets often had open sewers running down them. Epidemics spread quickly throughout the populations and killed many people. During the 1830s and 1840s there were massive waves of infectious diseases including scarlet fever, influenza, cholera, and typhoid.

These epidemics did not spare Verdi's loved ones. In rapid succession he lost first his daughter, Virginia, who died in the summer of 1838, then in October 1839 his son, Icilio. Next, their mother became ill with encephalitis, a brain infection for which there was no cure. Margherita died in June 1840. Verdi was heartbroken; his grief for his family overwhelmed him.

He returned to Busseto for Margherita's burial. Shortly after the funeral Verdi attempted to have his contract for a comic opera with Merelli annulled. When he left Milan he swore never to compose again. "My family has been destroyed, and in the midst of these trials I had to fulfill my engagement and write a comic opera! In a sudden moment of despondency I despaired of finding any comfort in my art and resolved to give up composing."

Merelli refused to annul the contract of the devastated composer. Verdi returned to Milan from Busseto two months after his wife's funeral to finish the opera and start rehearsals. It was very difficult for Verdi to compose a good comic opera while feeling so depressed. *Un giorno di regno* debuted in September 1840; the premiere was awful.

Before long, however, the very thing Verdi had wanted to shun in his grief—his music—would lift him up out of this dark period. ♣

Build a Water Purifier

CONTAMINATED WATER causes or contributes to many illnesses such as cholera, dysentery, and typhoid fever. Everyone needs unpolluted, pure water to drink. In the 19th century the lack of clean water caused the death of many children. We do not know which specific illnesses caused the deaths of Verdi's children, but contaminated water affected every family. Today, water treatment plants filter our water by taking out the impurities and adding chemicals to kill bacteria. Even a simple water purifier can filter particles out of water.

You'll Need

- Table
- Sturdy cardboard box at least 10 inches high, taped shut
- 2 large glass bowls, one containing 12 ounces water
- 2 tablespoons soil
- Spoon
- 1 yard of yarn

Place the cardboard box on the table, and place the bowl containing the water on top of the box. Carefully drop the soil into the bowl and gently stir the soil into the water.

Place the empty bowl directly on the table, next to the box.

Cut the yarn into thirds and braid the pieces together. Place one end of the yarn braid into the bottom of the bowl containing the water. Place the other end into the empty bowl so that the ends of the braid reach both bowls.

Wait about half an hour. What do you see in the empty bowl?

You should see only clear water in the formerly empty bowl; the yarn acted as a filter for the dirty water. Modern water purification plants use filters along with various chemical treatments to remove the elements that contaminate it and provide drinkable water.

A New Beginning

1841–1846

"Nabucco was racing a mad course through my brain."

—Giuseppe Verdi

❧

$\mathcal{V}$ ERDI RECOUNTED THE story of how he was drawn back to music and out of his deep depression. He said he happened to meet Bartolomeo Merelli, who was on his way to La Scala. Heavy snow was falling around them as the impresario handed the composer a libretto by Solera and asked him if he would just glance through it. Verdi took the text to his lodging but had no intention of even opening the manuscript. By his own account,

I came into my room and threw the manuscript angrily on the writing table. I stood for
a while motionless before it. The book had opened when I threw it down. My eyes fell on
the page and I read the line Va pensiero sull' ali dorate [Go my thought on golden wings].
Resolved as I was never to write again, I stifled my emotion, closed the book, went to bed,

Verdi holding the score to Nabucco.

Lebrecht Music & Arts Photo Library, Photographers Direct

and snuffed out the candle I tried to sleep but Nabucco was racing a mad course through my brain.

He gave up, sleep now was impossible; Verdi read the libretto several times that night. The next day he went to see Merelli.

"Isn't it beautiful?" Merelli inquired.

"Very beautiful," the composer answered.

"Well then, set it to music!"

Merelli stuffed the manuscript into Verdi's coat pocket and pushead him out the door. Verdi sat down and began composing when he reached his lodgings. "One day one line, another day another, here a note and there a phrase and little by little the opera was composed."

Nabucco occupied the composer through the autumn of 1841. The name of the work is a shortened form of the Italian name Nabucodonosor, the Babylonian king who is known in English as Nebuchadnezzar. *Nabucco* was based on the Biblical story of Nebuchadnezzar, who destroyed Jerusalem and took many of the captive Jews back to Babylon as slaves, including Jehoiachim, the king of Judah.

The Voice of Italy

ONCE THE score for *Nabucco* was completed the opera needed to be scheduled for pro-duction; it was to debut on March 9, 1842. The cast that was assembled for the premiere included the **baritone** Giorgio Ronconi for the title role. Ronconi was known for his acting abilities. Verdi was pleased that he was available; however, he was dismayed that the role of Abigaille, Nabucco's adopted daughter, had been offered to Giuseppina Strepponi. Although this gifted **soprano** had helped get *Oberto* staged at La Scala and had been one of his earliest supporters, Verdi had written the role of Abigaille for a very versatile soprano voice. He thought that this particular **diva** (literally translated as "goddess"; word for a female opera star) was aging and perhaps reaching the end of her operatic career. When Strepponi arrived for rehearsals Verdi was dismayed to discover that she was not feeling very well and this was evident in her vocal performance.

It had been a tradition in Italian opera that the composer rehearse with all of the performers and conduct the first three presentations of his work. As Verdi sat at the piano and rehearsed the cast of *Nabucco*, he must have been worried about the reception of the opera. His pupil Emanuele Muzio later described his teacher conducting during a rehearsal: "He shouts like a desperate man, stamps his feet as though he were playing the pedals on an organ, sweats so that drops fall on the score."

Learn to Read Music

WRITING MUSIC is capturing sounds on paper. Learning how to read music allows you to understand and perform a written piece. At first, it seems as if you are learning a foreign language, but once you master the basics it gets easier.

You'll Need
∞ Paper   ∞ Pencil

1. Music is written in notes that are placed on five lines and spaces called a staff.

2. Each staff has a clef, a symbol placed at the beginning of the staff that indicates the **pitch** (highness or lowness) in which the notes are written. Higher pitches are written on a treble clef, which is also called the G clef as it circles the second line on the staff, which indicates G.

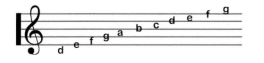

3. Lower pitches are written on a bass clef where the two dots indicate the fourth line is the F note.

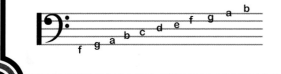

4. The **key signature** at the beginning of the staff indicates the key or the tone in which the music was written. It tells you which notes will be **sharp** or **flat**.

5. A flat is played a semitone (half a tone) lower than it would otherwise be played, while sharp is played a semitone higher. A note without a flat or sharp symbol is called a **natural**.

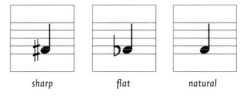

sharp   flat   natural

6. The **time signature** is indicated at the beginning of the staff. This tells you how many beats are in a measure and which type of note gets one beat.

7. Notes have time values— the amount of time assigned to each note. A whole note can be divided into half notes, quarter notes, eighth notes, and so on up to a sixty-fourth note.

whole note   half note   quarter note   eighth note   sixteenth note

8. A measure or a bar line contains a specific amount of time and is indicated by a vertical line that separates it from the next measure and mark sections of the music.

standard   double   end   begin repeat   end repeat   begin and end repeat

This is the language of music. Once you can read and write it, you can compose.

Try the following match-up to test what you have learned. Draw lines to match each symbol with its definition. Be sure to copy the page if you are using a library book

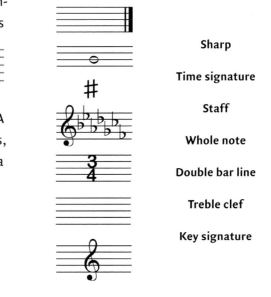

Sharp

Time signature

Staff

Whole note

Double bar line

Treble clef

Key signature

Design a CD Cover for Nabucco

A CD cover should attract people who are considering buying the music on the disk it contains. You can design a cover for *Nabucco* that will intrigue people and make them want to listen to the opera. The powerful words of "Va pensiero sull' ali dorate" ("The Chorus of the Hebrew Slaves"), from the third act of the opera, inspired Verdi to compose the work; listen to it to inspire your design.

Fly, my thought, on wings of gold
go alight on the slopes and the inclines,
where the warm and soft breezes
of our native land smell fragrant.

Greet the banks of the Jordan
and Zion's fallen towers.
Oh, my country so beautiful and so lost!
Oh, remembrance so dear and so lethal.

Golden harp of the prophetic bards,
why do you hang silent from the willows?
Renew our memories in our breast
that speak to us of times gone by.

Mindful of the fate of Jerusalem,
give forth a sound of harsh lamentation.
May the Lord inspire you a harmony of voices
which might instill virtue to our suffering.

You'll Need

∞ A music-listening device (such as an iPod, computer, or CD player)
∞ A download or CD of "Va pensiero sull' ali dorate"
∞ Pencil
∞ Scratch paper
∞ Ruler
∞ A sheet of sketchbook paper
∞ Colored markers or poster paints

Listen to "Va pensiero sull' ali dorate" several times. What thoughts do you have while hearing the chorus? What does it make you picture in your mind?

On the scratch paper sketch a few ideas for a central image you would like to use. After you have decided on the image, plan the lettering you will use for the title of the work, the composer's name, featured singers, the name of the orchestra and conductor.

Measure a 5- by 4-½-inch rectangle on the sketchbook paper and cut it out to create the CD cover.

First use the ruler to draw pencil lines for the writing and add your text, leaving space for your central image.

Then transfer your image design to the sketchbook paper. Color the design with the markers or paints. Let it dry.

Slip your CD cover into a CD case.

Verdi wanted everything to go perfectly; he put his whole being into the music. The premiere of *Nabucco* exceeded Verdi's dreams. The opera was an instant success; the audience went wild with applause. Merelli quickly increased the number of scheduled performances for *Nabucco*; he knew this opera was a moneymaker for La Scala!

Italian Nationalism

THE SUCCESS of *Nabucco* wasn't due solely to Verdi's arduous rehearsals. The opera appealed to the patriots who wanted Italy united. The Italian people were not alone in this quest. During the 19th century many countries were being ruled by foreign powers. A wave of nationalism

A drawing of the character Nabucco by the Italian artist Salvatore Fiume. Lebrecht Music & Arts Photo Library Photographers Direct

OPERA REHEARSALS

A rehearsal is a practice session before a performance. A conductor keeps the musicians working together. He or she reads the score, which contains the information about the piece of music including the key, **tempo** (the speed of the music), and the written notes. Every conductor adds his or her own interpretation of the music and decides how this work will be presented. He or she must convey this vision to the orchestra and other performers to be able to mold them into a coordinated group.

While musicians must pay close attention to the conductor, at the same time they must be aware of the instruments surrounding them so that their sounds can blend together. Soloists and ensembles need to follow the lead of the conductor for a flawless show. A rehearsal is an opportunity to work out any misunderstandings between the performers and the conductor.

An opera also must be staged; the performers work out their movements and positions on the stage (called blocking) and the lighting, backgrounds, and **props** (the items used by performers on stage) must be planned. A dress rehearsal is a full run-through of the work to be presented. This last rehearsal involves all of the staging, lighting, scenery, costumes, and props needed for the actual performance.

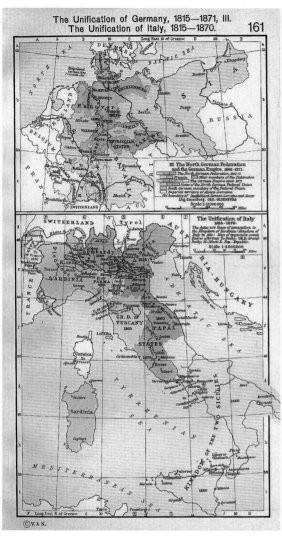

Map of treaty adjustments resulting from the Congress of Vienna. Courtesy of the University of Texas Libraries, The University of Texas at Austin

was sweeping the continent. Many revolutions were fought as one nation after the other was able to achieve independence. Watching this happen in other parts of Europe, the Italian people dreamed of reuniting their lands under one flag and with a constitution granting the citizens liberty and rights.

From the time that Romulus Augustulus, the last Roman emperor, was defeated in 476 CE, the people of Italy had been under the domination of foreign rulers including the Germans, the Spanish, and the French. All of these invaders had forcibly taken the land; it had been divided over and over.

Verdi's mother had hidden with her baby from the soldiers in the church bell tower during the last months of Napoleonic Wars. Napoleon had conquered Italy in 1796 and was finally defeated in 1815. The victors of the war against Napoleon—Great Britain, Austria, Prussia, and Russia—assembled at a conference known as the Congress of Vienna, where they redrew the political map of Western Europe. These nations made the decision to restore Italy to its former Austrian rulers.

Austria regained control of the northern half of Italy; the remainder of the people were to be under the authority of other countries and leaders, creating a hodgepodge of states. While the Austrians ruled over Lombardy, Veneto, and Tuscany, the Spanish governed Naples and Sicily. The pope wielded power over Papal States in Umbria and the Marshes. Only Piedmont preserved its Italian identity. These rulers dictated the rules and treated the citizens as if they were members of a colony supplying goods to the "mother country."

This restoration inflamed the Italian people, who raised the banner of *il Risorgimento* (The Resurgence) to fight for their goals. The *Risorgimento* led to a series of political events that eventually freed the Italian states from their foreign domination and united them politically. But it would prove to be a long battle.

From the start, Verdi identified himself with the cause of the *Risorgimento*, and the people of Italy perceived this in his music. The Milanese audience that went wild over *Nabucco* had identified with the conquered Hebrews depicted in the opera. They viewed the Austrian authorities as the Babylonians and saw themselves as the Jewish slaves. "Va, pensiero," the chorus of the Hebrew slaves, became the unofficial anthem of the *il Risorgimento* revolutionary movement. The people of Italy had found a voice for their aspiration of reunification in the music of Giuseppe Verdi. Various revolutionary groups arose to achieve this goal, including a faction known as the Carbonari.

Every Italian anxiously waited for the various revolutionary groups to accomplish their objective. Verdi, always an avid reader, followed the political scene by reading the newspapers daily. He also read the pamphlets and books published by the revolutionary leaders. His love of his homeland and hopes that it would become independent can be gleaned from the "*Risorgimento* operas" Verdi composed in the 1840s. After *Nabucco*, audiences attending *I Lombardi* identified with the Italian Lombards and saw the opposing Saracens as the oppressive Austrians. Verdi's *La battaglia di Legnano* was written in response to and in support of the 1848 series of revolutions led by Mazzini. Several Italian opera composers of that period were involved in the growing patriotism of their compatriots. Gioacchino Rossini, Gaetano Donizetti, and Vincenzo Bellini had written operas that represented the culture and traditions of their people. These **bel canto** (beautiful singing) composers were very popular in Italy.

THE CARBONARI AND YOUNG ITALY

A secret political society known as the Carbonari (the charcoal burners) was determined to force the Austrian emperor Ferdinand I to grant rights to the Italians. This society had been founded early in the 19th century with the objective of overthrowing the current rulers and creating a unified country. The leaders of the Carbonari were intellectuals and landowners who wanted the authorities to respond to their demands for more representation and freedoms.

The members of the Carbonari were spread throughout the country. In 1820 the Carbonari revolted in Naples; another uprising occurred in Piedmont in 1821. The major demand of this revolutionary group was a constitutional government. The Austrian authorities quickly put down the rebellions. The Carbonari had to wait for another opportunity to overthrow the foreign rulers.

The arts played a key role in the development of Italian political and cultural awareness. Writers expressed the goals of unity and freedom in their works; their novels and poetry inspired the populace to join in rebellion. A member of the Carbonari, the philosopher Carlo Cattaneo, founded his own journal, *Il Politecnico* (The Polytechnic), through which he urged changes in official policy.

The writer Giuseppe Mazzini, another member of the secret society, was so disheartened by the failure of the Carbonari to overthrow the government in 1821 that he always dressed in black as a sign of mourning over his disappointment. Mazzini was imprisoned for his views and then forced to leave Italy. From exile he founded the political movement Young Italy with the aim to release the country from foreign oppression and install a republican form of government. In 1833 the Austrians stated that membership in Young Italy was treason and, therefore, punishable by death.

Bel canto is a singing style that emphasizes the importance of the voice in opera. This style of vocal technique was first used in the 17th century by singers to showcase their voices. It was embraced by Italian opera singers until it was considered to be "old-fashioned" in the 19th century. The bel canto librettists had to always be mindful to select words that would allow the singers' voices to flow lightly and smoothly with the music. Gioacchino Rossini (1792–1868) was a leading composer promoting bel canto. *Guillaume Tell (William Tell)*, dated 1829, is Rossini's final opera and depicted the tale of the 14th-century Swiss patriot.

The melodious bel canto score of *Anna Bolena* thrust Gaetano Donizetti (1797–1848) into the spotlight. This two-act opera was based on the story of Anne Boleyn, the second wife of Henry VIII of England. Donizetti tailored his operas to audiences, providing them with tunes they could easily sing. For years Donizetti was very prolific; he could write an opera in a week, and he actually produced 73.

Vincenzo Bellini (1801–1835) is considered by many to have composed the ultimate bel canto work with *Norma*. The tragic two-act work is more intense than the typical bel canto opera. The aria "Casta diva" became one of the most memorable arias of the 19th century.

The bel canto era spanned most of the 18th century but reached its peak in the middle of the 19th century, then slowly gave way to the dictates of the Romantic era. The composers of bel canto works left a lush legacy for future composers.

The nationalists would not give up their dream of having their own country. When a new and supposedly more liberal pope was elected in 1846, four years after the premiere of *Nabucco*, their hopes and expectations rose. Soon after his election Pope Pius IX declared an amnesty for the radical leaders of the *Risorgimento* and for others who had been imprisoned for political crimes. The new pontiff also promoted expanding the railroad system, creating an agricultural college, and some other progressive ideas. The Austrian rulers watched these developments closely.

Like all Italians, Verdi was constantly monitoring the political scene. As the revolutionary groups made their attempts to gain independence, his hopes and expectations rose. Verdi became increasingly disappointed as he observed all of the efforts to create a liberated Italy fail. His music had become a symbol for the revolution, giving expression and inspiration to the groups fighting to achieve this end. As one rebellion after the other did not succeed, a depressed Verdi retreated into his composing and tended to his investments. ❧

Make a Clay Map of Italy

ITALY IS located in central Europe. Part of the country is a peninsula that extends out into the Mediterranean Sea. Sicily, the largest island in the Mediterranean, is found at the southwestern tip of Italy. Sardinia is the second largest island in the Mediterranean and is located closer to North Africa than it is to Italy. A map of Italy will help you picture the various places where Verdi lived.

Adult supervision required if using oven

You'll Need

∞ Map of Italy
∞ Tracing paper
∞ Pencil
∞ ½ cup salt
∞ 2 cups flour
∞ ¾ cup water
∞ 1 tablespoon cooking oil
∞ Medium-sized mixing bowl
∞ Spoon
∞ Disposable aluminum baking pan
∞ Cuticle stick
∞ Oven (and potholders) or sunshine
∞ Permanent marker

1. With the pencil, copy the outline of the map of Italy on the tracing paper.

2. Mix salt and flour together in the bowl. Add enough water to get a nice claylike consistency while stirring the mixture with the spoon.

3. Keep stirring while adding the oil.

4. When the mixture is the consistency of clay, pick it up and transfer it to the aluminum baking pan.

5. Press the clay about ¾ inches thick into the pan; smooth out the surface with your hand.

6. Place the tracing paper outline on the clay. Use the cuticle stick to draw the outline of your map on the clay. Press hard but do not cut all the way through the clay.

7. If you are using sunshine, set the pan in the sun to bake and set for about three hours. If you are using an oven, preheat the oven to 250° F and place the pan in the oven for one hour.

8. Carefully remove the pan from the oven with potholders.

9. When the map is baked and cool, use the marker to write the major cities and island names on the clay. Refer back to the map on page 2 to label the smaller towns Roncole and Busseto.

Tracing Paper

Baking Pan

Cuticle Stick

CRIES FOR LIBERTY

1847–1853

"The man who trusts men will make fewer

mistakes than he who distrusts them."

—Count Camillo Benso di Cavour

⁓

IN 1847, VERDI took his first voyage out of Italy. After a brief visit to Switzerland he went to London for the premiere of *I masnadieri* (The Bandits) in Her Majesty's Theatre. The management of the London theater had paid a handsome sum to the composer for *I masnadieri*, which showcased one of the most famous sopranos in Europe at the time. The "Swedish Nightingale," Jenny Lind, was to perform the role of the orphan Amalia; her voice was celebrated worldwide.

All of British society turned out for the debut of *I masnadieri*; Queen Victoria was the guest of honor. The women in their magnificent gowns and the men in their formal attire politely waited for the first notes to open the four-act work. Applause followed the sad ending. The opera was well liked in London, yet Verdi did not feel comfortable there; he did not wish to return to the city in the near future. Verdi found his stay in London to be "like living on a steamer" due to its fog and climate. He also did not care for the prim and proper manners of the British, finding that they "do not suit us Italians."

JENNY LIND

Johanna Maria Lind was born in Stockholm, Sweden, in 1820. Her unmarried parents were not able to provide a comfortable and stable home so the infant was sent to live with a foster family in the Swedish countryside. Three years later Jenny returned to her parents' home, where her mother was running a day school for girls. At the age of nine the child's excellent voice gained her a place in the Stockholm Conservatory of Music. Nine years later she debuted in Carl Maria von Weber's opera *Der Freischütz*. She was an instant success.

After further study in Paris and Berlin, Lind began a European tour that elevated her to stardom. She toured the United States from 1850 to 1852 with the assistance of the American showman and entertainer P. T. Barnum. Lind donated a large portion of the money she had made during her American tour to charity. When the American concerts ended, Lind married the pianist Otto Goldschmidt in Boston; they had three children. Lind-Goldschmidt became a teacher at the Royal College of Music in Sweden. She was as well known for her charitable work as she was as a **coloratura** (a soprano with a high and nimble voice who can sing with **ornamentation** and **embellishment**). Her last concert was held in 1870; Lind died in England in 1887.

Soprano Jenny Lind c. 1850.
Library of Congress LC-DIG-pga-03992

City of Lights, Liberty, and Love

LEAVING ENGLAND, Verdi headed to France, where the Paris Opéra wanted one of his operas. The contract for *Jérusalem* (a rewriting of *I Lombardi*) was negotiated in early 1847. Verdi arrived in Paris that November for the premiere with his former student Emanuele Muzio, who had completed his studies and had decided to remain alongside his former teacher to assist him. He explained that his studies with Verdi had led to friendship: "Always together at lunch, at the coffee house, playing together (for one hour, from twelve to one); in short, he goes nowhere without me."

The revised *I Lombardi* had been translated into French and renamed *Jérusalem*, and details had been altered to appeal to the French taste. A mandatory ballet had to be added and other revisions were made to adapt the music to the French language. Much had to be accomplished in the five months before the debut, but Verdi was dismayed by the quality of the musicians. "I have never heard worse singers or a more mediocre chorus," he is quoted as saying shortly after his arrival in Paris.

But Verdi knew that having this opera performed outside of Italy was a big step. He would be better paid, since in his native land he received only one payment for an opera while in France he could receive a royalty on each performance. Most important, his works would be exposed to new audiences.

Verdi had found much to appreciate in Paris. He was surrounded by many artists and thinkers; he was not buttonholed on the streets by an adoring public and could go about his daily activities with few interruptions. The French citizens enjoyed freedoms unavailable in Italy; people spoke freely without the fear of being arrested, and they appeared to be less judgmental of other people's choices. Censorship did not have a role in the arts. The newspapers were allowed to print their opinions and authors could publish shocking works. Soon Verdi was able to read and converse in French. Each day he read the Parisian newspaper *Fígaro*, a habit he continued in Italy during his later years.

During this journey outside of his homeland Verdi also became reacquainted with the singer Giuseppina Strepponi, who was very attracted to his music. Strepponi had been born in Lodi in 1815 to a family of musicians. The soprano had studied at the conservatory of Milan. Verdi had first met Strepponi in 1839 when she was

Sing Like a Diva

IF YOU like to sing there are ways to improve your ability to generate a better sound. Producing a great singing voice takes more than talent—it takes practice. Many parts of the body are involved, from your brain to your diaphragm. Remember never to strain your voice by forcing it to sing out of **range** (the lowest and highest notes that your voice can produce). Practice four days a week in 20-minute sessions.

You'll Need
∞ A music-listening device (such as an iPod, CD player, or computer)
∞ Computer with a printer
∞ Aria of your choice from a Verdi opera
∞ Printout of the lyrics of the aria
∞ Full-length mirror
∞ Tape recorder

Listen to the aria, noting how the singer projects his or her voice. When does the singer take a breath? Listen to the phrasing of the words.

Stand in front of the mirror and adjust your posture: stand up straight with your shoulders down and with one foot slightly in front of the other. This gives you the best posture for projecting your voice.

Relax to allow your lungs to expand and contract. Practice diaphragmatic breathing by inhaling fully and slowly letting the air escape. Do this twice before you sing. (You can place your hands on your midsection and feel the diaphragm expand).

Warm up your voice by singing solfeggio (the notes of the scale with do, re, mi) or vowel sounds. Begin softly and then add to the volume.

When you are familiar with the music, sing the aria. Tape yourself and save the recording. Practice for three months and tape yourself again. How do the performances compare?

the darling of Milan and Verdi an unknown composer. It was her influence with the impresario of Milan's famous opera house, La Scala, that had convinced him to stage *Oberto*, his first opera. During the terrible years when Verdi dealt with the death of his children and his wife, Margherita, Strepponi's friendship had been a great comfort to the grieving young composer.

Now, seven years after that tragic loss, the 34-year-old composer and the soprano (two years his junior) fell in love, and the couple moved in together in Paris. Their cohabitation did not seem to be an issue in France (as it would be later when they returned to Italy). Strepponi provided the composer with companionship and would prove to be an enormous help in Verdi's work. Her contacts and stature had helped Verdi when he first began composing operas. She listened to his ideas and made inspired and creative suggestions. As a trained musician she had an excellent ear and valuable experience as an opera singer.

Giuseppina Strepponi.

A Chance at Liberty

VERDI WAS still enjoying life in Paris in March 1848 when an uprising in Milan drove the Austrians out of the city. From France, he wrote, "Honor to all Italy which at this moment is truly great! The hour has sounded—make no mistake—of her liberation. It is the people that wills it, and when the people wills there is no absolute power that can resist."

Hopeful that his countrymen could now achieve their freedom, the composer rushed home. He was thrilled that Italian independence seemed to be around the corner. He wrote to his librettist, Francesco Maria Piave, "You talk of music to me!! What are you thinking of? Do you think I want to concern

COUNT CAMILLO BENSO DI CAVOUR

Count Camillo Benso di Cavour (1810–1861) was from an aristocratic family. He attended a military school and served in the engineering corps of the Piedmont-Sardinian army until he resigned in 1831. The next year he became the mayor of Grinzane, the town where his family had an estate. Cavour traveled to Switzerland, France, and England to learn about the political and social reforms in these countries, their economies, and their agricultural progress. Impressed by the social and political changes that had given citizens more liberties, he returned to Italy convinced that such reforms were desperately needed there. He was elected to the Piedmont Parliament in 1848.

In 1852 Cavour became prime minister and minister of foreign affairs of Piedmont. In this position he attempted to modernize the local political and financial conditions. To promote trade, he entered into treaties with Belgium, England, and other European countries. Cavour sought improvements in the infrastructure; he initiated projects to benefit and expand the economic life of his region.

myself now with notes and sounds? There is and should be only one kind of music pleasing to the ears of the Italians in 1848—the music of the guns!"

King Charles Albert of Sardinia declared war against the Austrians and urged his army to drive the foreigners out of Italy. At first, it seemed that the rebellious forces were winning, but then the Austrian military rallied and was able to drive the opposition back. When the rebellions failed, Verdi was once again despondent. He wrote, "Force still rules the world! And justice? What good is it against bayonets? We can only weep over our misfortunes and curse the authors of so much disaster."

By the middle of 1849, Austria was back in control. King Charles Albert abdicated, allowing his son, Vittorio Emanuele II, to succeed him. A constitutional government survived only in Piedmont, where Count Camillo Benso di Cavour, a new leader of the Italian rebellion, lived.

Rebellion and Censorship

WHILE THE rebellions in Italy had failed to lead to independence, Verdi was able to express his political frustrations and opinions through music, composing his only overtly nationalistic opera, *La battalia di Legnano* (The Battle of Legnano). Verdi knew that this opera would stir up the people; he wanted them to continue to press for independence. The subject of the opera was a revolt by the cities of northern Italy against the 12th-century Holy Roman Emperor Frederick Barbarossa. This subject could easily be interpreted to mirror current events.

The four-act work, based on a French play, was scheduled to open in Rome on January 27, 1849. A large number of people had come to the dress rehearsal and heard the words of support for the 12th-century revolutionary movement; in their imaginations they projected the words of the opera ahead a few centuries into the present. The dress rehearsal audience went wild, but their reaction was rather subdued in comparison to the crowd attending the premiere—it demanded that the entire last act be repeated. Soon after the debut, the censors decided that *La battaglia di Legnano* was not to be performed again.

Verdi composed a number of operas that further added to the public's cries for independence and liberty: *I Lombardi alla prima crociata* (The Lombards on the First Crusade), *Ernani*, *I due Foscari* (The Two Foscari), *Giovanna d'Arco* (Joan of Arc), and *Attila*. In the choruses

A statue of Count Camillo Benso di Cavour Monument in Milan. Library of Congress LC-USZ62-103329

of these works, the people heard messages for Italian patriots and freedom fighters, even though they may not have been there. The operas excited the audiences and displeased the censors. The authorities watched audiences with distrust; they feared that a performance could erupt into a political protest. They also kept a tight lid on the content of a work, always searching for perceived moral, political, or religious offenses. Composers and librettists had to submit their work to the censors for approval before works could be staged.

Verdi had encountered few problems with the censors before the revolutions in 1848. Nonetheless, all of Verdi's operas written in the 1840s are described by historians as "*Risorgimento* operas" because they caused the people to imagine revolutionary ideas were hidden in the works. The authorities also became more vigilant as unrest spread among the populace.

Several years earlier, during an 1843 rehearsal of *I Lombardi* in La Scala, the archbishop of Milan had become alarmed when he heard that the opera would contain a religious procession, a baptism, and the prayer "Ave Maria." The church feared that this prayer was being used to make a political statement. The archbishop sent the police to intervene and avoid a scandal. The composer refused to make any major changes to the opera but did make a concession: "Ave Maria" became "Salve Maria." The public loved the opera, which Verdi later revised for the French opera. The audiences especially responded to the act 4 chorus "O Signore, dal tetto nation" ("O Lord, You did not call us"), which they believed sent a revolutionary message like the one in "Va, pensiero."

At this time Verdi also ran into problems with the political censors who were watching

Pope Pius IX, sitting on a throne at center, with various members of the clergy behind him.

for material that they believed to be objectionable or revolutionary. Religious references in artistic works were also inspected. In Italy the Vatican's religious censors kept a vigilant eye for any deviation from the accepted doctrines of the Catholic church. Verdi did not agree with any type of censorship of artistic works and fought the interference in his operas.

The Vatican often questioned Verdi's moral and religious choices. But the reaction of an audience to a text cannot be determined beforehand. When the Italians attending *Nabucco* decided that the circumstances of the Hebrew slaves reflected their own enslavement by Austria, the censors, who had approved the opera, were astounded. When the audiences attending *Attila* heard Ezio, the Roman general, stating to Attila that he can "have the whole world as long as he, Ezio, can rule Italy," the attendees also perceived a resemblance to their political situation. After performances of *Attila* Verdi would be accompanied home by cheering crowds and even brass bands.

Although the plots of the operas contained characters from the past and had no connection to the current political events, the audiences read between the lines and viewed the historical scenes as though they were comments on the contemporary situation. All of Verdi's operas were interpreted as depicting battles against tyranny; demonstrations usually followed performances or even broke out during the shows.

Problems with censorship continued to plague Verdi. A battle over a new opera began when he elected to base the work on the play *Le roi s'amuse* (The king amuses himself) by Victor Hugo. Twenty years before, when the drama opened in Paris, Hugo faced problems because the censors believed that the play was immoral and disrespectful to the king. This had been a sensitive issue for the French authorities. The play had been banned by the French censors in Paris long before Verdi chose it to be the source of his latest opera. He knew he would be facing the same predicament that Hugo had encountered, but the controversial drama appealed to him, and Verdi never was one to give in to a system he believed was irrational and unfair.

Originally titled *La maledizione* (The curse), the opera was contracted to open in Venice in 1851. The title of the work was later changed to the name of the court jester, *Rigoletto*. Verdi was not surprised to learn that the military governor was unhappy with the heavy subject of the opera and wanted changes to be made. Afraid that the work would be banned, Verdi wrote to Piave, his librettist, "As soon as you receive this letter, start moving: run throughout the city, and find an influential person who can obtain permission to do *Le roi s'amuse*. Don't sleep. Stir yourself. Hurry."

The opera related the story of a sweet, innocent young girl being duped by an evil and dishonest member of the nobility with the help of Rigoletto, the court jester. The immorality and power of the authorities as depicted in the plot was seen by the public as a real-life threat in the 19th century.

Piave assured the composer that the subject of the opera would be approved, but Verdi was still worried. He knew that the censors could cause problems; once again he voiced his concerns when he wrote,

The suspicion that Le roi s'amuse may be forbidden creates serious embarrassment for me. I was assured by Piave that there was no obstacle to this subject, and trusting his word, I set myself to study it and ponder it profoundly, and the idea, the musical color had been found in my mind. I could say that the main, most toilsome part of the job was done. If I were now obliged to think about another subject, I would lack the time for such study, and I could not write an opera that would satisfy my conscience.

As the premiere approached, the censors were adamant that the work displayed "disgusting immorality." Verdi maintained that the opera had taken shape and that it was too late to significantly alter the work. On December 1, 1850, Verdi was informed that *Le roi s'amuse* had

been prohibited. He was agitated and blamed the librettist. "The decree refusing it plunges me into despair, because now it is too late to choose another libretto, which it would be impossible, quite impossible for me to set for the winter."

Meanwhile, in order to save the work that had been completed, Piave quickly attempted to refashion the libretto into something more acceptable for the censors. But Verdi would not give in. Although Piave made significant changes to the libretto to accommodate the demands of the censors, Verdi was very angry about the censorship and refused to budge. The censors objected to the jester being portrayed as deformed and ugly. In a letter Verdi insisted that the jester had to remain as the text presented him and that this was essential to the opera:

Putting on the stage a character who is grossly deformed and absurd but inwardly passionate and full of love is precisely what I feel to be so fine. I chose this subject precisely for these qualities, those original traits, and if they are taken away I can no longer write music for it.

Any negative portraits of royalty were seen as an insult or a threat to the monarchy. The censors and Verdi had to negotiate a compromise. The setting of the drama was moved from France to Mantua, a duchy not under Austrian

Italian opera star Titta Ruffo as Rigoletto, 1912.

control that the notorious Gonzaga family had ruled for centuries. It was also agreed that all of the historical characters in Hugo's play were to be given Italian names. This change satisfied the authorities and *Rigoletto* was approved for performance.

Verdi's gift for **melody,** or the tunefulness of the music, was evident in this opera; the audiences were swept away by the music, and the aria "La donna é mobile" ("Woman is fickle") became one of the most beloved **tenor** arias ever composed. The composer was thrilled with the success of *Rigoletto*. In a letter dated 1853 he stated, "As far as dramatic effectiveness is concerned, it seems to me the best material I have yet put to music."

Verdi c. 1850.

The Middle Period

By the 1850s Verdi had become the most popular Italian opera composer in Europe. He was now well paid for the **productions** of his works and began to invest some of the money he was earning into land and real estate in Italy. The composer could have retired at this point in his career, but he was not interested in a leisurely life; over the next few years he was very productive.

Verdi had composed 16 operas in 11 years. The pace was hectic and the composer referred to these as his "years in the galley." Due to the stress and pressures of deadlines, his health was often poor, but he was always looking for the next project. Verdi suffered from overwork and had little time for rest.

With *Rigoletto* Verdi had entered what music scholars call his "middle period." In June 1851 the composer was working on his two upcoming operas. Planning the design of each work took time and energy. The plots, characters, acts, scenes, and music had to be worked out. When *Rigoletto* had been well received in its 1851 premiere, Verdi had immediately thought of a sequel to the work; the plot was based on the drama *El trovador*, by Antonio García Gutiérrez. The composer was still in Venice enjoying the success of *Rigoletto* when he wrote to a librettist and playwright he had worked with and admired, Salvatore Cammarano, to ask if he would be interested in another collaboration. The distinguished writer expressed interest in the new venture. Cammarano, a native of Naples, was a good choice. The librettist was very respected in that city and the opera was due to premiere there in the Teatro San Carlo.

The composer had written a first draft of the plot before he asked the librettist to take over. Verdi envisioned that this opera would include an unconventional female character; he wanted the main role to be a vengeful gypsy named Azucena. Roma culture was viewed as strange and controversial in Europe. Verdi liked to add an element of surprise into his operas—in *Il trovatore* this was to be the character of Azucena. At first, he had wanted to title his opera *La zingara* (The gypsy) or *La vendetta* (The revenge) before deciding on *Il trovatore* (The troubadour).

Cammarano worked on the text but did not seem to agree with Verdi's choice of a Roma woman as a major character in the opera. Cammarano and Verdi had disagreed during previous collaborations, and Verdi had allowed Cammarano's opinions to prevail. Verdi felt that the librettist overly adapted controversial

Il trovatore poster c. 1936.
Library of Congress LC-USZC2-5405

THE ROMANI PEOPLE

Believed to have originally come from northern India over 1,000 years ago, the group of people sometimes called "gypsies" is found throughout the world. The word "gypsy" was derived from the mistaken idea that they came out of Egypt. The people of this community call themselves Romani, which also refers to their language. The dark-skinned Romani speak their own language, practice their own religion, and follow a nomadic lifestyle that has subjected them to prejudice by people who fear them because of their differences. This intolerance peaked during World War II when at least a quarter million Romani were murdered in Hitler's death camps.

During their travels the Romani have traditionally made a living through the sales of wares they produce, seasonal farm work, horse trading, and tinkering. As superstition led people to believe that gypsies had magical powers, the women often resorted to fortune telling. The Romani are also known for their music. Their musicians were famous for their virtuosity on their instruments, which included violins, accordions, panpipes, and guitars. Frequently, singing and dancing were accented by hand clapping and tambourines. Many classical composers have been inspired by Romani music.

Make a Panpipe

IN ANCIENT Greece the instruments called panpipes were associated with the god Pan. They were made out of cane, reeds, bamboo, or clay. Panpipes are folk instruments that are still popular in South America, Romania, and Asia.

Adult supervision required

You'll Need

∞ 3½ feet PVC tubing, ½ inch in diameter
∞ Ruler
∞ Marker
∞ Protective goggles
∞ Pipe cutter
∞ Sandpaper
∞ Duct tape
∞ 8 pennies

1. Measure the PVC tubing into the following lengths for each note: 6¾ inches for C, 6 inches for D, 5½ inches for E, 4¾ inches for F, 4¼ inches for G, 3¾ inches for A, 3½ inches for B, 3¼ inches for C. Use the marker to indicate where to cut the tubing as you measure.

2. Put on your protective goggles. Have an adult help cut the tubing into the measured pieces with the pipe cutter.

3. Use sandpaper to smooth out the cut edges. Wear the goggles to keep the dust out of your eyes. Clean off any dust remaining on the pipes.

4. Cut a piece of tape that is twice the width of all the pipes. Place the tape on a table with the sticky side up and lay the pipes across the tape in order of size, from longest pipe (lowest note) to shortest pipe (highest note), keeping the tops lined up evenly. Fasten the tape around the pipes.

6. Tape a penny to the bottom of each pipe to seal the holes.

7. Blow across the tops of the pipe to make sounds.

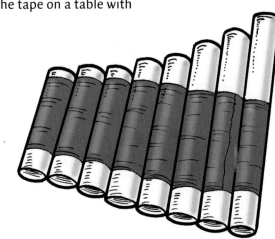

subjects to please the censors rather than face a battle with them. This time, Verdi felt compelled to insist on his viewpoint. He respectfully told the older and acclaimed librettist that he had to blame himself since they had not come to a full agreement about the project before beginning to put the opera together. Verdi was determined to have a controversial woman as the main character of this work. The librettist finally agreed.

Cammarano shortened Antonio García Gutiérrez's original *El trovador*—a huge dramatic work set during the 15th-century Spanish Civil War. Unfortunately, in July 1852, Cammarano died before completing the libretto. Verdi quickly made arrangements for Cammarano's widow to be taken care of now that her husband was gone; then he began to look for a suitable person to take over the libretto.

Only two acts had been completed when Verdi asked Leone Emanuele Bardare, a young poet from Naples, to finish the text. Bardare expanded the role of the lady in waiting, Leonora, making her character equal to the role of Azucena. Verdi was pleased that the main female roles in the work now balanced each other.

Il trovatore's debut was a definite triumph. The music critic of the weekly journal *Gazzetta Musicale* wrote, "The public listened to every number with religious silence and broke out with applause at each interval. The end of the third act and the entire fourth act aroused such enthusiasm and their repetition was demanded."

The opera opens without an **overture**, or orchestral introduction; instead a series of arpeggios (broken chords) and horn calls are heard to start unraveling a dark story about passions and revenge. Verdi's theatrical and romantic instincts are demonstrated in *Il trovatore*'s spirited and rousing "Anvil Chorus" in act 2, scene 1, which contrasts with the chorus and duet of the dramatic "Miserere" scene where the words "Lord, thy mercy on this soul" set the dark mood in act 4. The opera quickly became one of Verdi's most popular works. Over the next three years it had 229 performances throughout Europe.

In contrast to *Il trovatore*, when *La traviata* (The fallen woman) premiered in the same year, there was a different outcome. The operas had opened only seven weeks apart—*Il trovatore* in Rome on January 19 and *La traviata* on March 6, 1853, in Venice. Both works were romantic **melodramas** (a dramatic work with exaggerated emotions), and both had been composed while Verdi was troubled. He was always close to his parents, and the recent, unexpected death of his mother caused him great pain. He was also disturbed by some financial decisions at this time. He had purchased properties that had put him into debt, and owing money worried him.

Even though the need to continue to work on *Il trovatore* hindered the composing of *La traviata*, Verdi sought to have the opera ready by the contracted date. He was determined to honor his commitments. The libretto was penned by Verdi's friend and now frequent collaborator Piave. *La traviata* told a tragic tale based on *La Dame aux camélias* (The Lady of the camellias) by the French dramatist Alexandre Dumas Jr. (the son of the famous author of *The Three Musketeers*). The novel had been adapted for the stage, and Verdi and Strepponi went to see it in Paris in 1852.

During the second half of the 19th century artists began to depict everyday life in their art. They began to select subjects that dealt with reality instead of historical or mythological themes. The stark plot of *La Dame aux camélias* reflected this interest in realism. The controversial realism of the play enticed Verdi, who wrote to a friend that the subject of the opera was "a subject for our time."

The composer always wanted his operas to be well accepted by his audiences; he dreaded any failures. His many letters give us insight into his thoughts: "In the theater lengthy is synonymous with boring. And of all styles boring is the worst.... The artist must look into the future, perceive new worlds amid the chaos."

La traviata was swiftly put together, but it certainly was not boring. None of Verdi's operas before *La traviata* had a contemporary setting. The work depicted real people in a real-life situation with a flawed female lead dying of tuberculosis, a dreaded but common disease at the time. It had scenes depicting people gambling and consorting with this main character, named Violetta, who was a courtesan. In the 19th century these taboo subjects were shocking and scandalous. Verdi even wished to set the work in the present day with contemporary clothing, but the owners of the opera house begged him not to do so.

A few months before *La traviata*'s premiere the composer had threatened to stop work on the opera unless Fanny Salvini-Donatelli, the **prima donna** (principal female singer) who had been chosen to sing the lead role of Violetta, was replaced by someone younger, thinner, and more delicate in appearance. He wanted a diva with a frail appearance that would have suited the role of a sickly, dying heroine better. Piave rushed to Busseto to convince Verdi to go along with the agreements that had been made. The librettist had his hands full. Verdi was in a terrible mood, but in the end the composer gave in. The selected soprano would perform.

Verdi predicted that *La traviata* would not be well received. He was right. The day after the premiere, Verdi wrote to his assistant, "Was it my fault or the singers'? Time will tell." The audience did not care for Salvini-Donatelli singing the female lead; they sneered at her performance. The critics were astounded by the realism of the opera and the portrayal of a courtesan as the heroine.

The composer withdrew the work so that he could make revisions. In this opera Verdi had boldly expanded the depiction of the characters, making them more lifelike. As Violetta dies in the final act, she sings only a few lines while gasping for breath. In previous operas, dying main characters still sang full arias as they expired. The other main roles in *La traviata* also are more three-dimensional than was usual in the past, and their arias reflect their personalities.

The opera was not a big hit until a year later, when the changes were made and a new diva sang the role of Violetta. The composer gave credit to the younger and slimmer coloratura Maria Spezia-Aldighieri for her part in making the opera a sensation. Subsequently *La traviata* was seen as a work with unforgettable melodies, waltzes, and characters. It was soon performed in many countries with great success. ❦

A LOVE STORY

1853–1859

"We are still the whole world to each other."

—Giuseppina Strepponi Verdi

~

*V*ERDI WAS RECEIVING a steady income from his operas, money that he could plow back into the farmlands he now owned. In 1848, when Verdi had bought the land located about two miles outside of Busseto, it was in poor condition. He built a large new manor house there and oversaw all the construction details. Verdi relished being in charge and always believed that he needed to take control of any event or situation that arose. When construction was complete, Verdi and Giuseppina Strepponi settled in to the new house, which they named Sant'Agata.

Next Verdi turned his attention to improving his own land as well as that of his fellow farmers in the region. He bought modern, steam-powered machines and taught his tenant farmers how to farm more efficiently using newly developed methods.

Verdi employed many people to maintain Sant'Agata with its extensive gardens and to work on his farm. The composer took an active role in the management of his large estates. He usually awoke at five o'clock in the morning to check on his crops and animals before breakfast. He oversaw various large projects, such as excavating canals for drainage and constructing roads that the farmers could use to bring their produce to market. He bought threshing machines powered by steam and modern plows to till the fields. The improvements benefited

A steam-powered threshing machine.
Library of Congress LC-USF33-006595-M3

AGRICULTURE IN MID-19TH-CENTURY ITALY

In Italy during the mid-19th century most peasant farmers were still using traditional methods to work their lands. The rice, wheat, and other grains grown in the Po Valley were harvested by hands wielding the sharp blades of sickles and scythes—the ancient method. Although steam-driven harvest machines had been invented, they were too expensive for the small Italian farmer. Horses and other domesticated animals pulled their plows.

The fruits and olives of the warmer and drier southern climate were often fertilized with manure gathered from the other animals on the farm. Grapes, which were grown in most of Italy, were watered by primitive irrigation methods that involved hand pumping the water to the vineyards.

It took many farmers to feed the people who lived in cities; as populations grew, the need for more efficient and productive

farming was evident. Modern agricultural techniques were being developed and new crops were being planted; these improvements were slowly implemented by the small farmers of Italy. Pesticides, fertilizers, and advanced techniques increased crop production. As machine-powered irrigation systems and farming machinery became more affordable and available to the small farmer, their hard physical labor was lessened.

Left: Sant'Agata, Verdi's home outside Busseto, Italy.

the farmers surrounding Busseto as well as people from the entire area near the village. Despite his busy life the composer made time to pursue hobbies such as quail hunting and collecting the autographs of the famous people he met on his travels or those who came to visit him.

March Toward War

IN THE rest of Italy beyond Verdi's sanctuary of Sant'Agata, the political situation was changing at a snail's pace. Verdi had closely watched the unrest growing during the *Ris-*

orgimento years. He had followed the political attempts at uniting his country and believed that Count Cavour's policies could make an impact. He was growing impatient with the progress of the fight for independence. In a letter to Clarina Maffei, the wife of his friend the poet Andrea Maffei, Verdi wrote, "Where is the longed for independence of Italy that we have been promised?"

Other countries in Europe were heading toward war. In the summer of 1853 Russia had taken over an area that had been under the control of Turkey, France, and England. The territory that Russia had occupied was Crimea,

Map of Crimea. Courtesy of Susan Silberman

located on the Crimean Peninsula, which juts out into the Black Sea south of Ukraine.

Turkey declared war against the Russians in October; the French and British demanded that Russian troops be pulled back. The Russians ignored the ultimatum, so France and Great Britain joined Turkey's battle. The kingdom of Sardinia became involved when King Vittorio Emanuele II sent soldiers to aid the French and British. The assistance of the Sardinians in winning the Crimean War allowed the Italians to take part in the peace negotiations held in 1856 after the Russian defeat. At the negotiating table with the French and British powers, the seekers of Italian independence would be able to present their case.

THE CRIMEAN WAR

The Crimean War was the first war to be reported in newspapers and to be photographed. Daily reports were published in the *Times* keeping the British public aware of the events. Some unexpected developments grew out of the conflict. News of wounded soldiers being treated in horribly inadequate conditions caused the establishment of better practices of field medicine. Florence Nightingale, a British nurse, improved the treatment of the injured soldiers.

New inventions such as the telegraph facilitated communication. A more stable bullet had been invented, which increased the range and accuracy of rifles. For the first time soldiers dug trenches to protect themselves, and newer military tactics were tried.

Off the battlefield other developments took longer to implement. The British system of selling the right to be a military officer to men in the "correct social class" was re-evaluated and abolished. Russian serfs, who were peasants tied to the land of an aristocrat, were set free in 1861. The Russian tzar, Alexander II, realized that serfs, forced to fight for a cause that did not matter to them, were no match for free men fighting for something that they believed in.

A hospital ward during the Crimean War. Library of Congress LC-USZC4-10261

"So Well Matched"

IN 1845 the residents of Busseto had considered building a theater, but the budget would not allow it. Almost 20 years later, the people of the village decided it was time to build one, and the municipality was ready to begin construction. Verdi argued that the theater was a wasteful enterprise that the town could not afford to erect and maintain.

This difference in opinion created a sharp debate between the composer and the citizens of Busseto. Some of the bitterness that arose between them must also have been due to the treatment that Giuseppina Strepponi received from the people in the small town. They had ignored her in church and when she was out shopping. Removing themselves from the hostile stares of the gossips was a major reason for the couple's move out of Busseto to the safe haven they built at Sant'Agata.

Verdi was also incensed over a letter he had received from Antonio Barezzi, his former father-in-law. Although the letter has not survived, it must have made comments about the composer living with a woman to whom he was not married. In a letter responding to Barezzi, Verdi made the statement,

In my house there lives a lady free, independent, a lover like myself of solitude, like myself pos-
sessing a fortune that shelters her from all need. Neither I nor she owes anyone an account of our actions. . . . Who knows whether or not she is my wife? And if she is, who knows what the particular reasons are for not making the fact public? . . . In my house she is entitled to as much respect as myself—even more.

Strepponi's devotion to the composer was evident in her letters to him when he traveled to opera houses to oversee his works. In one letter to Verdi, when he was in Venice, she had written,

We are still the whole world to each other. . . . As long as God gives us good health, our simple and modest pleasures and desires will cheer and comfort us even in old age; our affection and characters, so well matched, will leave no room for those frequent and bitter fights which diminish love and end by destroying every illusion.

After 12 years together, the composer and Strepponi were finally married in the village of Collonges-sous-Salève in southeastern France in 1859. The ceremony was held in the parish church and was kept secret. They were wed far away from the people who had disapproved of them in Busseto. Even Verdi's father, a strict Catholic, had voiced his disappointment over their choice to live together without being

Write a Letter to Someone You Admire

IT IS rare to write or to receive a letter today due to e-mail and other electronic methods of correspondence. Letter writing is an art that was cultivated for centuries. In fact for many years it was the only way to communicate with people far away. Handwritten letters are a much more personal and friendly form of communication; to be able to hold a piece of paper in your hand that was penned by someone who took the time to write it is a tangible and lasting gift.

You'll Need

- ∞ Scratch paper
- ∞ Pen
- ∞ Letter-size stationery
- ∞ Stationery envelope
- ∞ Stamp

Select a friend, relative, teacher, or someone you admire, then find a comfortable place to work.

1. Make a list on the scratch paper of things you admire and appreciate about this person (he's kind to people who need help; she's funny and quick to make a joke). Write down some examples of how he or she displayed these attributes (he helped me with my math homework; she told me a funny story once when I was feeling sad). Then add the reasons why you admire these personal qualities (helping others makes the world a better place; being funny makes everyone around you feel good).

May 9, 2013

Dear Julia,

I want to tell you how much you mean to me. You are my big sister and do lots of nice things that make me happy. If I am stuck on a math problem you patiently explain what I need to do. You politely listen to my piano practice and applaud, even when I make mistakes. The best thing you do for me is when you brush my hair and tell me it's pretty.

I think you are the best big sister any girl could have. I love you even when I stick out my tongue at you. You just laugh and call me silly.

Sincerely,

Jeanie

---

2. Organize your list by the most important to the less important things you like about the recipient.

3. Using your best handwriting, begin your letter on the stationery with the date, if you choose, or with the word "Dear" followed by the recipient's name and a comma. Write your letter, incorporating the thoughts and ideas on your scratch paper and keeping in mind sentence and paragraph structure.

4. End your letter with a complimentary closing such as "Sincerely," or "Yours truly." Sign your name under the closing, fold the stationery into thirds, and place it into the envelope. Write the recipient's name and address on the front and center of the envelope; write your address on the top left portion of the envelope.

5. Place the appropriate postage on the top right corner of the envelope and drop it in the mail. Now await a happy and surprised reaction!

sanctioned by the church. Strepponi was deeply hurt by the scorn of the villagers, and she felt isolated when she remained at home while Verdi was away. Verdi understood her dismay; he wrote to one of his friends sarcastically commenting on the attitude displayed by the people of Busseto, "How beautiful, how elegant! What a place! What society!"

In the letter Verdi wrote to Barezzi, he had penned an even nastier commentary, calling Busseto "a town where people have the bad habit of prying into other people's affairs and disapproving of everything that does not conform to their own ideas." Verdi had ended this letter with the threat that he may decide to leave the Busseto area, even mentioning that he

OPERA HOUSES

A box at the Vienna State Opera.

Alexander Donchev / Shutterstock

The first commercial opera house opened in Venice in 1637. By 1850, all over the globe, many larger cities and some smaller towns were building them. Like any theater, the U-shaped auditoriums have seats facing the stage. Besides the seats in the center of the hall tiers of balconies climb up the walls; some of these balconies are enclosed to form boxes.

Many operas require the use of complex machinery such as elevators, revolving mechanisms, and overhead equipment to produce special effects. Stage crews operate lighting and other equipment and change the scenery using devices hidden in the stage ceiling. The orchestra pit, which houses the instruments and the conductor, normally is positioned in front of and below the stage.

Today many opera houses use technology that allows the audience to read a translation of the words that are being sung. In keeping with tradition, the majority of opera houses do not use any microphones or speakers on stage. For this reason, the acoustics of the theater are carefully planned and tested to allow the richness of the music to flood the hall.

Play Bocce Ball

BOCCE WAS played by the ancient Romans and is still an extremely popular game in Italy. It is similar to bowling except bocce is played outdoors on a flat, open space at least 10 feet wide and about 70 feet long. Bocce is played with eight large balls and one smaller ball called the *pallino*. It takes only a few minutes to learn the rules. The game can be played with two or four players.

You'll Need

∞ 2 or 4 players

∞ Set of bocce balls

∞ Flat area such as a lawn, a paved surface, or even the beach

∞ Towel

∞ Yardstick or tape measure

1. Point out the playing field to the players. Establish a starting line with the towel.

2. Divide players into two teams. Each team gets four balls of the same color divided equally among the players.

3. Choose a player to toss the *pallino* from the starting line into the center of the playing field. Everyone else stands outside the playing field.

4. The player who tossed the *pallino* gets the first toss from the starting line for one of the bocce balls, trying to throw it as close as possible to the *pallino* without touching it.

5. Each player on the opposing team now takes a turn from the starting line to toss one bocce ball closer to the *pallino* than the starting player's ball.

6. If no one from the opposing team gets a bocce ball closer to the *pallino* than the starting player did, each team member of the starting team gets a turn in an attempt to do so. Use the yardstick or tape measure to measure the distance.

7. Rotate teams until all eight bocce balls have been used.

8. The team with the closest bocce ball is given one point for each of its balls that is closer to the *pallino* than the other team's closest ball. Any bocce balls that are at an equal distance from the *pallino* or touching the *pallino* do not gain points.

9. The team that gets the most points begins the next round, where the attempts are repeated until one team wins with a score of 13 points.

still resented the fact that they had not entirely welcomed him as the church organist so many years before. But this was basically an empty threat since the composer had intense ties to the area where he had purchased his land.

The couple had put a great deal of money and effort into their estate at Sant'Agata, and that is where they decided to remain. The rambling manor house suited their needs and the lush gardens provided the perfect haven for reflection or for entertaining their frequent guests. Perhaps on the lawn a game of bocce would be played.

A Masked Ball

DESPITE SPENDING so much time farming, Verdi continued to compose, being careful to set aside hours each day to work on his scores. His wife was always nearby to help him think through any rough spot that he encountered. Working at his writing desk in Sant'Agata was peaceful and pleasant; Verdi enjoyed taking brief breaks from his labors in his lovely gardens. The couple scheduled visitors when Verdi did not have work that demanded his full concentration and lots of his time.

He had completed an opera for the San Carlo Theater in Naples to debut during the winter carnival season but did not approve of the singers who were available to perform the work, so it was postponed. According to the censors in Naples this opera had to be completely altered, and Verdi had to comply with their many demands. The playwright, Antonio Somma, had no prior experience writing libretti. Based on a true story, the opera was originally titled *Gustavo III*, based on the name of the Swedish king Gustavus Adolphus, who was killed in 1792 while attending a masked ball. The Austrian authorities were nervous about allowing a monarch's assassination to be depicted on stage during a time of public unrest. Just as rehearsals for the opera began, an Italian nationalist had attempted to kill the French emperor Napoleon III and the Duke of Parma had recently been assassinated.

The opera was renamed, the main character was transformed into a duke, and the work was set earlier in history. These alterations to the work still did not satisfy the censors; they wanted even more changed. Now Verdi got stubborn; he would not agree to make any more changes. Instead, the opera would be offered to a theater in Rome.

In Rome Verdi discovered that once again he could not satisfy the censors. Verdi wrote to Somma, "I'm in a sea of troubles! It is almost certain that the censors will forbid our libretto. Why, I don't know." For the rest of the demands, Verdi and Somma came up with a plan—reset

Make a Carnival Mask

VERDI SET *Un ballo* at a carnival, or *carnevale* in Italian. Various cities around the world hold these winter festivals that mark the beginning of the 40-day fast before Easter. People often wear elaborate costumes and masks. Carnival masks are constructed out of many materials and decorated with elaborate artwork and embellishments such as ribbons, feathers, or beads. Masks made out of papier-mâché are easy and fun to make.

Adult supervision required

You'll Need

- Pile of old newspapers
- Water
- 2 large bowls
- Measuring cup
- White glue
- Balloon
- Acrylic paints
- Feathers, glitter, etc. for decorating
- Marker
- Craft knife
- Tape
- 6-inch dowel

1. Cover your work surface with some of the newspapers to protect it.

2. Tear (do not cut) other newspapers into strips about 1 inch wide by 6 inches long. Place them in a bowl with warm water to soak for five minutes.

3. Use the measuring cup to mix two parts glue with one part water in a bowl.

4. Blow up the balloon to roughly the size of your face; tie it with a knot.

5. Gently press the water out of a strip of newspaper and cover it with the glue mixture. Stick the newspaper strip horizontally on the side of the balloon facing you and smooth it down with your fingers. Repeat these steps, with strips placed horizontally and their edges overlapping, until the side of the balloon is covered.

6. Continue with more strips now placed vertically, overlapping the edges until all the horizontal strips are covered, forming a mask shape on one side of the balloon. Tuck the ends of the strips of newspaper under the edges of the forming mask.

7. Let the first layer dry completely. Now add another layer, again starting with the strips going in a horizontal direction. Then add the vertical strips. Remember to tuck the ends of the strips under to create smooth edges to your mask.

8. Repeat the process, creating a third layer. Let it dry completely.

9. Pop the balloon and pull it out. You will be left with a masklike shape.

10. Hold up the mask to your face. Using the marker, note where holes need to be cut for your eyes. With the mask on your work table, cut out ovals with the craft knife using the marks as guides.

11. Paint and decorate the mask.

12. When the decoration is completed, attach the dowel securely with tape to one edge of the mask.

13. Hold the mask in place by grasping the dowel in your hand.

Newspaper

Balloon

the opera in a place and time that the censors would not find threatening. In protest to the absurd demands of the censors, the librettist would not allow his real name to appear on the published libretto; in its place an anagram of his name was used, therefore, Antonio Somma became Tommaso Anoni.

The final title given to the opera was *Un ballo in maschera* (A Masked Ball). On opening night the audience must have been somewhat confused and dumbfounded by the notion that the stage was filled with characters singing in Italian while attending a *carnevale* in the American colony of Boston, Massachusetts! ♣

Carnival mask.

VIVA V.E.R.D.I.

1860–1869

"I offer neither pay, nor quarters, nor food;
I offer only hunger, thirst, forced marches, battles and death.
Let him who loves his country with his heart,
and not merely with his lips, follow me."

—Giuseppe Garibaldi, Italian patriot

ANOTHER BATTLE WAS being fought for independence; this time France joined Piedmont-Sardinia in its struggle against Austria. The people in Italy who wanted reunification were hopeful that an alliance with the French emperor Louis Napoleon Bonaparte, known as Napoleon III, would be very helpful. Napoleon III was the nephew of the Napoleon who had been king of Italy; this monarch had spent much of his childhood in Rome. In 1848 he became the president of the French Third Republic; four years later he was proclaimed as the emperor of the French.

Napoleon III.
Library of Congress LC-USZ62-131393

65

The prime minister of Piedmont-Sardinia, Camillo Benso di Cavour, had turned to Napoleon III for his assistance in expelling the Austrian rulers. Cavour had engineered the Italian partnership with the French and the British during the Crimean War. This cooperation during the Crimean conflict was noted by Napoleon III, but he also had his own reasons for bringing the French army back to Italian soil—he wished to expand the influence of

General Giuseppe Garibaldi.
Library of Congress LC-DIG-pga-02437

GIUSEPPE GARIBALDI

Giuseppe Garibaldi fervently believed in an independent Italy. His family lived on the coast of Piedmont-Sardinia. His father and grandfather were seamen; the young man became a sailor and later a captain in the merchant marines. In 1833 Garibaldi met Giuseppe Mazzini and joined the Young Italy movement and the Carbonari revolutionaries. By 1834 he had taken part in an insurrection in Piedmont and had to escape when the revolt failed. Although he was not captured, a court sentenced him to death for his participation in the rebellion.

In 1836 he fled to South America, soon joining a revolt against the Brazilian government. During this conflict he met Anita, a woman fighting alongside him. They married and had four children. Garibaldi also fought in Uruguay when Argentina attempted to retake the country. For these exploits he earned the nickname "Hero of Two Worlds."

He and his volunteer soldiers were famous for their valor and for wearing red shirts, which became Garibaldi's symbol. Garibaldi returned to Italy in 1848 but once again he was forced to flee, this time to the United States, where he became a citizen. He returned to Italy in 1860, just in time to rejoin the battle that led to independence.

Giuseppe Garibaldi entering Naples, 1860. Library of Congress LC-DIG-pga-02437

his country throughout Europe and perhaps to gain more territory for France. Napoleon III and Cavour made a deal: if the French helped in the struggle for Italian independence France could have Nice and Savoy while Italy retained Lombardy and Venetia.

In 1858 Napoleon III met secretly with Cavour and the two men concocted a plan. They agreed to a treaty by which France would go to the aid of Piedmont in the event of Austrian aggression. Therefore, if Cavour could make the Austrians appear to have started a war against the Italian patriots, Napoleon would send his armies to fight by their side. They also talked about the division of Italy if this latest clash with the Austrians was won.

Hundreds of Italian volunteers rushed to the kingdom of Piedmont-Sardinia while Cavour attempted to provoke Austria to attack. An Austrian ultimatum warning the Italian people against the impending conflict was issued. The French deemed this ultimatum to be an aggressive act and quickly dispatched their troops to fight the Austrians.

Giuseppe Garibaldi (1807–1882) was an Italian patriot who took an active role in the struggle for independence. Garibaldi first led a force to Sicily, where he engaged the Austrians in battle; next his army marched into Naples. He also expected to fight for and conquer Rome to make it the capital of a united Italy.

Composer Turned Politician

AT THE beginning of the war against Austria, Verdi had been very excited. In a letter to his friend Clarina Maffei he wrote that he would have joined the fight himself if he had been younger and in better health. At the age of 45, the composer explained, "My head won't stand five minutes of sun, and a breath of wind or a touch of damp sends me to bed for weeks on end."

Although he was neither a political nor a military figure, Verdi was considered a champion of Italian patriots' cause. He had publicly expressed his thoughts and feelings many times. Back in 1848, during the uprisings, he had written to a friend, "The hour of liberation has struck, be sure of it. It's the people that want it and when the people want something, no absolute power can withstand them!"

It had taken much longer than anyone had imagined, but by 1860 the liberation appeared to actually be at hand. Toward the end of the Austrian rule, opera fans began to shout "Viva V.E.R.D.I.!" concealing a clever message within the composer's name: **V**iva Vittorio **E**manuele **R**e **D'I**talia ("Long live Vittorio Emanuele, king of Italy"). The patriotic fans shouting the phrase risked arrest as they were really promoting Vittorio Emanuele as the king of Italy though he was only the king of Sardinia. If they

Verdi in 1860.

were questioned by the authorities they would claim that they were simply expressing their appreciation for the composer.

In 1859 the Duchy of Parma, the territory where Verdi lived, had voted to join with Piedmont-Sardinia in the struggle for nationhood. Verdi had gone to the capital city of Turin as a member of a delegation to see Vittorio Emanuele II and to plead for the annexation of Parma by the only independent state in Italy at the time.

Before the battles were over, Cavour called for a creation of a parliament, a body of legislators who enact laws, similar to the US Congress. The prime minister insisted that Verdi, as a symbol of the spirit of the revolution, had to place his name on the ballot in this election. Verdi reluctantly agreed to run for Parliament

VITTORIO EMANUELE II

Vittorio Emanuele II (1820–1878) was the son of Charles Albert of Sardinia and Maria Theresa of Austria. In 1842 Vittorio Emanuele had married his Austrian first cousin Adelaide. Over 13 years the couple had eight children before Adelaide died during childbirth. As the oldest son Vittorio Emanuele inherited the Sardinian throne when his father abdicated in 1849 after a war with Austria. The king was able to negotiate a largely favorable peace treaty and upheld the constitution that his father had granted to the people so that Sardinia remained the only state in Italy with a constitution.

He wisely appointed Count Cavour as the prime minister, allowing the economy of the region to flourish. As a well-liked and respected monarch, Vittorio Emanuele II was viewed as the type of king the Italian people would welcome to lead them; thus, the king of Sardinia became a symbol of *il Risor-*

King Vittorio Emanuele II, engraving in The Leisure Hour *magazine, 1880.*

Shutterstock

The coat of arms of the kingdom of Sardinia.

Oleg Golovnev / Shutterstock

gimento. When in 1861 the unification of Italy was proclaimed, Vittorio Emanuele became the first king. He requested to retain his title as Vittorio Emanuele II instead of Vittorio Emanuele I of Italy. The constitution of 1848 was extended to the rest of the country.

People reaching Florence from Tuscany to vote for the annexation of Parma to the Italian State, from the Journal Universel, *1860.* Shutterstock

with the understanding that if he won he would insist on his right to resign from the legislative body as soon as the Italian state was firmly established. He was willing to serve his people, but he also wanted to be able to return to his peaceful life as a farmer.

Verdi had not had much time to compose in the previous two years while he tended to his estate and entered politics; he had even commented to his friends that he had stopped being a composer. But in 1860 Verdi received a commission for a new opera and was able to return

Debate and Vote on an Issue

VOTING IS a right guaranteed by the US Constitution to all American citizens over the age of 18; many people think that voting is an important privilege. Countless people all over the world do not have this right. Voting is not confined to elections of local, state, or national representatives—it can also be used to discover how the majority wants issues to be resolved. There are issues that are important to all citizens who may not be old enough to vote in an election but they can still make their opinions count. You and your classmates or friends can hold a vigorous debate and then vote about something that concerns all of you.

You'll Need
∞ Issue to vote on (such as the value of recycling, school dress codes, constructing a neighborhood park, or requesting changes to the school cafeteria menu)
∞ 1 or more other people to present the opposing side of the issue
∞ A place for debating the issue (such as your classroom, club, or living room)
∞ People to vote (friends, relatives, classmates, members of a club)
∞ Paper
∞ Pens
∞ Shoe box or paper bag

Here are some tips for conducting a debate:

1. Clearly identify the issue to be debated.

2. Research the topic for facts.

3. Keep notes on your sources of the facts.

4. Write down any quotes you might use and their source.

5. Establish a team strategy and debate what position you will take. Outline your argument.

6. Decide who will present the material.

7. Set up or make certain you know the debating rules, such as how much time each side has to present or to argue their side.

8. Make sure that each person involved in the debate is aware of his or her role.

9. Arrange a place, date, and time for a public debate and voting.

10. Create the ballots for voting: list the choices or simply have a place to check off yes or no.

11. Hold the debate. Then hand out the ballots and pens for a vote, have the ballots collected and counted, then announce the result.

to his music. At the same time he continued to attend to his political campaign, winning the election to Parliament in 1861 as Garibaldi prepared his army to march toward Rome.

Political leaders determined that Italy was to be united under the same constitutional monarchy that had been established in Piedmont-Sardinia under the same monarch, Vittorio Emanuele II. The new state would be missing two pieces: Venetia, which remained under Austrian control until 1866, and Rome, which was still a possession of the Papal State. Before the new country could be proclaimed, Cavour

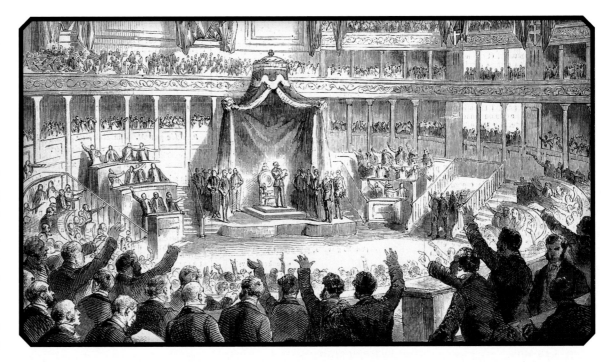

King Vittorio Emanuele II opening the Italian Parliament, 1860. Antonio Abrignani / Shutterstock

THE FLAG OF ITALY

The Italian flag is called *il Tricolore* in Italian, referring to its three colors. The three bands of equal size on a rectangle begin with the green followed by the white in the center and the red on the right. It is believed that originally the colors came from the colors of the uniforms of the militia of Milan.

There are several interpretations of the meaning of the flag's colors. One version asserts that the green symbolizes the vegetation of the countryside, the white stands for the mountains, while the red represents the blood of those who fought for Italian unification. Another explanation is that the green stands for hope, the white for faith, and the red represents charity.

Many variations of the flag were adopted in different historical periods. During Napoleon's rule the Napoleonic Eagle was placed on a field of green and centered in the flag. Coats of arms were added and removed and horizontal bands became vertical. Throughout the makeovers, the variations of the flag symbolized the transformations that comprised the history of the Italian people.

Design and Sew a Flag

A FLAG may be the emblem of a nation or a way to signal an idea. Royalty, military corps, ships, schools, corporations, and others have used flags to distinguish themselves, display their nationality, signal orders, or to herald their presence. The distinctive design and color of a flag identifies its purpose. Designing and sewing your own flag is a way to display your creativity.

You'll Need

- Scratch paper
- Pencil
- Crayons
- Ruler
- ½ yard of a solid-color fabric (in the color you choose)
- Straight pins
- Needles
- Thread
- 2 snap-on grommets (available in hardware or craft stores)
- Scissors
- Dressmaker's carbon paper (available at fabric stores)
- Old towel
- Fabric markers

1. Decide on the emblem you want on your flag and sketch out your ideas on the scratch paper with the pencil.

2. Use the crayons to fill in the colors of the emblem.

3. Use the ruler and pencil to measure and draw one line ¼ inch and one line ½ inch from the edges along the two longer sides and one of the shorter sides of the fabric. These marks indicate where to turn the fabric under to form a hem.

4. Turn the edges under on the first ¼ inch line drawn from the edge of the fabric and then turn this under another time on the ½ inch line. Pin in place.

5. The remaining shorter edge will be the band for the grommets; measure and draw one line ¼ inch and one line 3 inches from this edge. Turn in on the lines and pin.

6. Measure out about 24 inches of thread, then thread the needle, knot the thread, and sew the hems in place on the back of the flag.

7. Mark the position of the two grommets on the side of the flag: one should be placed 1 inch from the top and the other 1 inch from the bottom.

8. Using the template that comes with the grommets, mark the holes with the pencil.

9. Cut out the holes with the scissors. Attach the grommets to the flag.

10. Place the dressmaker's carbon on the front of the flag in the center and top it with your sketch of the emblem.

11. Outline the sketch with a pencil to transfer it to the fabric. Remove the papers.

12. Cover your work surface with an old towel.

13. Using the fabric markers, paint the emblem.

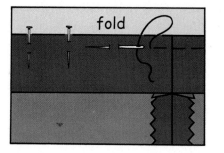

died. Verdi was grief stricken. As a member of Parliament, Verdi took part in the vote that made Italy an independent nation. On March 17, 1861, the Kingdom of Italy was announced.

Vittorio Emanuele II was crowned as the king of Italy by the Parliament on the day it began meeting, and the various states were joined together. Venetia would be annexed five years later. Rome became the new capital in 1872. The flag of Italy was based on a red and white flag that had long been a symbol of Milan. The tricolor flag of the French inspired the addition of a third bar in green. Over time, the Italian flag went through many design changes until the Republic of Italy was declared.

Verdi was out of the country for much of the time while the details of the new government of Italy were worked out in Parliament. He and Giuseppina, whom he affectionately called Peppina, journeyed to Russia for the debut of a new opera. Stopping in Moscow on his way to St. Petersburg, the composer and his wife attended a production of *Il trovatore*. After the opera Verdi exclaimed, "If you go to India and to the interior of Africa you will hear *Il trovatore!*"

"A Peasant from Roncole"

FOLLOWING THE trip to Russia the couple went to Paris for almost a year. They then jour-

---

VERDI'S PRIMA DONNAS

The soprano Marianna Barbieri-Nini (1818–1887) performed in many of Verdi's early works. Her initial debut at La Scala in 1840 had been a disaster, so she returned to her hometown of Florence, where she made a second debut. This time her premiere was a huge improvement. The diva was famous for her powerful voice and dramatic presentations.

Fanny Salvini-Donatelli (1815–1891) was well regarded for her flexible and expressive voice; she undertook many roles in Verdi operas. She sang the role of Violetta at the premiere of *La traviata*, a fiasco because she lacked the frail body that the role required.

Teresa Stolz (1834–1902), a native of Bohemia, was a soprano recognized for her remarkable voice and acting ability. She had studied in Prague before launching her career in Italy. Verdi sometimes insisted that she be cast in his operas.

Giuseppina Pasqua (1855–1930) began her career as a soprano but then trained for and accepted roles as a **mezzo-soprano**. Her talent led to tremendous fame throughout Europe. She was known for her extensive repertory.

---

neyed to Madrid in Spain. The couple returned to their home at Sant'Agata, which was commonly known as Villa Verdi.

In 1865 Verdi withdrew from the Parliament. He always pictured himself as a man of the soil, a farmer. This was the image Verdi wanted to project to the world. Whenever he was interviewed by a journalist he depicted himself as coming from an uneducated peasant background and returning to his roots on the land. Although he knew that his parents had not been simple peasants—they had owned land and were

Giuseppe Verdi Place, Busseto, Italy. Shutterstock

tradespeople—he enjoyed telling others that he was "a peasant from Roncole ... just a peasant, rough hewn, and I have never been able to express an opinion worth two pence."

In Busseto the people had completed their long-sought-after theater and wished to name it the Teatro Giuseppe Verdi in Verdi's honor. Of course, they also were certain that the man

74

honored by having the theater named after him would contribute money toward its upkeep and provide works to be performed there. Verdi had not supported the idea of building the theater but reluctantly agreed that they could name it in his honor, and he also provided a sizeable donation.

But the insults and gossip over so many years had affected Verdi's feelings about the people of Busseto; he stated that he would never set foot in this theater. The couple insulated themselves at their estate. Giuseppina wrote, "Giuseppe Verdi who has filled the world with the glory of his music the citizens of Busseto have rewarded by poisoning his life with every sort of vileness."

In 1867 the composer's ailing father passed away, followed by the death of Antonio Barezzi six months later. Verdi mourned for both of his "fathers." His father, his aunt, and his orphaned great-niece, Filomena Maria, had been residing in a house in Busseto that Verdi owned. The seven-year-old was a pleasant and loving child whom Verdi loved deeply. Now in their fifties, Giuseppi and Giuseppina decided to adopt the young girl they called Maria. The following year Maria was legally their daughter and living at Sant'Agata. The solitude of their lives was broken by occasional guests, mainly from the music world, and their travels to oversee the inauguration of new operas. ❧

Aida

1870–1879

*"I do not write my notes at random
but try to give them a definite character."*

—Giuseppe Verdi

IN 1870, AS a new decade began, the Papal States were finally incorporated into Italy, the Franco-Prussian War started, and the opening of the Suez Canal was celebrated. Unfortunately, as the years progressed, Verdi's patience grew shorter and his temper grew hotter. He was someone who needed to feel in control, and he was disgruntled with many things in his life, in music, and in Europe. Verdi told his friend the impresario Mauro Corticelli, "Let no one else be master, trust nobody." In addition, he informed Corticelli, "I am absolutely resolved to put everyone in his place and make everything run well."

His wife had found it more and more difficult to deal with his sudden outbursts of anger; the slightest thing could upset him and send him into a rage. Giuseppina was not sure how to respond or how to react to these outbursts of temper. Their marriage was damaged by his behavior. She had commented, "I don't know with what words and in what tone of voice I am to speak to him, so as not to offend him!"

CLAUDIO MONTEVERDI

Claudio Monteverdi (1567–1643) was born in Cremona, a town in northern Italy. He worked for the court of Mantua as a conductor, viol player, singer, and composer. In 1607 he was asked to compose an opera for the annual carnival of Mantua. Having composed madrigals (songs that tell a story), he had a clear understanding of how to combine music and text in an opera, the new art form that had been created and developed during the Baroque era. Monteverdi was inventive with this new musical genre. His *L'Orfeo favola in musica* (Orpheus Legend in Music) is considered to be a milestone in the development of opera.

Monteverdi wrote about a dozen operas. Sadly, most were lost over time and only three remain. The surviving operas display Monteverdi's ability to merge the music and the text to depict the drama. His works are unique in comparison with the other operas composed during the same time frame, and they display the art of a genius. These remaining operas have been incorporated into the **repertoire,** or body of works, of today's opera companies. Monteverdi had a tremendous influence on the direction that this new lyric drama would take in the future.

The composer bought more land and built houses for tenants who paid rent to him for the land they farmed. Verdi continued to carefully supervise his accounts, his many servants, and his home and garden in addition to these farms. He oversaw all of the farm workers, always insisting that they use the most modern methods of fertilization, crop rotation, and irrigation. He purchased a steam-powered engine from England to water his fields. He built up the banks of the Po River to avoid flooding. Nothing was too trivial for his attention.

In his spare time Verdi enjoyed reading, especially the classics written by the ancient Greek dramatists and the works of William Shakespeare. He also kept up with what was occurring in music and the theaters. It was very important to the composer that the heritage of Italian opera continue along the unbroken lines begun by Claudio Monteverdi in the 17th century.

Since the 1860s Verdi had found it difficult to find suitable subjects for his operas. People made suggestions, but the composer was not easy to please. He searched hard for a text that appealed to him enough so that he could set it to music. In 1865 Shakespeare's play was the basis for a revised version of his 1847 opera *Macbeth;* the audiences and critics did not like the altered work. One critic actually stated that Verdi did not understand Shakespeare. The composer had responded, "It may be that I have not done justice to *Macbeth* but that I don't know or understand or feel Shakespeare—no, by God, no. He is one of my favorite poets; I've had him in my hands since my earliest youth and I read him over and over again." Eventually, Verdi would turn to the bard again.

Spectacle in Egypt

The subject of Verdi's next work would be suggested by an unusual source in a faraway place. The Suez Canal was being finished in Egypt at the same time that a new opera house was being constructed in the capital city of Cairo. The viceroy (ruler) of Egypt admired Verdi's music and requested that the composer write a hymn for the festivities planned for the opening of the canal. Verdi turned down the request to compose a hymn, so the viceroy asked if the composer would instead write an opera for the new theater. Verdi agreed to this request.

The leader of Egypt wanted this opera to be based on the ancient culture of his country. August Mariette, a French Egyptologist who studied the ancient Egyptian civilization, suggested a story that he had made up. Verdi liked the plot of Mariette's story.

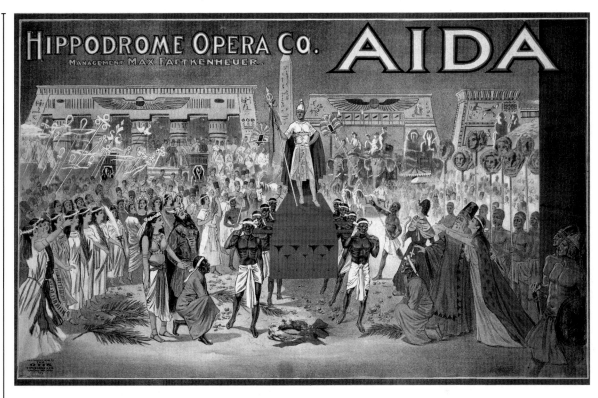

Aida *poster.* Library of Congress LC-USZC4-12407

Royalty gathered from all over the world to take part in the festivities celebrating the opening of the canal. Among the invited guests were the Austrian emperor, a prince and princess from Holland, and the king of Hungary. Since a French company had built the canal, for the Egyptian viceroy the most important royalty present was the Empress Eugénie, the wife of Napoleon III, who was to preside at the opening ceremony. For the comfort of the visiting French empress the leader of Egypt even had a special palace constructed on the Nile River.

Paint a Poster to Advertise *Aida*

Posters are both an artistic and informative way to let people know about an event. You can paint a poster advertising *Aida*. Designers and artists often need inspiration to do their best work. For your inspiration, listen to "Celeste Aida," the aria that Radames sings about his love for Aida. This work is cited as one of the best examples of a solo aria that Verdi ever composed.

You'll Need

∞ A CD or MP3 download of "Celeste Aida" from act 1 of *Aida*
∞ A music-listening device (such as an iPod, computer, or CD player) or a computer with Internet access to YouTube
∞ Scratch paper
∞ Pencil
∞ Poster board
∞ Acrylic paints
∞ Paintbrush
∞ Water
∞ Markers

1. While listening to the aria, let images enter your thoughts and sketch them on the scratch paper.

2. Select the image that you feel is the best for a poster, and plan what the poster needs to say. Be sure to include all the details someone interested in attending would need to know (the title of the opera, composer, location, time, and so on).

3. Try out different lettering for the written information on your scratch paper.

4. Plan your poster, considering the placement of the image and written information and the paint colors that the music inspired.

5. When you are happy with your design plan, transfer it to the poster board in pencil. Paint the image with the acrylic paints, and fill in the lettering with the markers.

The fabulous festivities, feasts, and spectacles were attended by journalists who had come from countless countries to describe the opening of the Suez Canal in their newspapers. They reported that the engineering achievement was celebrated with many forms of entertainment including band concerts, dancers, fire eaters, and performances by Bedouin horsemen. Tents of yellow and red silk were erected to keep the sun off the thousands of people feasting inside them. It was grand party that lasted for three weeks.

Instead of composing for the opening of the Suez Canal, Verdi signed a contract to compose an opera for the newly constructed Cairo Opera House; he began to work on the four acts with the librettist Antonio Ghislanzoni based on the story supplied by the Egyptologist August Mariette. As they worked on the libretto and the score of the opera the cast was selected and the scenery and costumes were produced in Paris.

Opening festivities for the Suez Canal.
Library of Congress LC-USZ62-95900

THE SUEZ CANAL

The Suez Canal is a manmade, 101-mile-long waterway that was constructed over a period of 10 years. The canal provides the shortest maritime route between Europe and Asia. It connects the Mediterranean Sea and the Red Sea by separating the African continent from Asia, eliminating the need for ships to navigate around the African continent. The canal cuts the length of the trade route from Europe to Asia by 6,000 miles.

The construction of the canal was a huge engineering feat—millions of cubic tons

of earth had to be moved. A French company undertook the project and an international team of engineers drew up the plans. The initial work was done with shovels and pick axes until heavier machinery arrived from Europe. Progress on the construction was often held up by labor disputes. An epidemic of cholera caused the project to fall behind and added four years beyond the original completion date. When the canal finally opened, on November 17, 1869, a gigantic celebration, lasting many months, was held in Egypt.

The Suez Canal (between 1856 and 1860).
Library of Congress LC-DIG-ppmsca-04552

Create Pizza Party Invitations

EVERYONE ENJOYS a party. For your next occasion consider a party serving everyone's favorite Italian food: pizza. Start out with some delicious-looking invitations. Decide how many invitations you will need and duplicate the instructions until you have enough to invite your friends.

You'll Need

- ∞ Brown, red, and white construction paper
- ∞ Circle compass
- ∞ Scissors
- ∞ Glue
- ∞ Ruler
- ∞ White paper cut into 6- by 6-inch squares.
- ∞ Pen

1. Using the compass, draw a 10-inch circle on a brown piece of construction paper and cut it out.

2. Measure a 9-inch circle with the compass on a red piece of construction paper and cut it out.

3. Glue the red circles to the brown ones, leaving an inch of brown on the edges.

4. Cut some white construction paper into 10 strips that are about 2 inches long and ¼ inch wide to make the "mozzarella cheese." Glue these strips scattered around the red circle.

5. Write your party information on the squares of white paper. Be sure to include the date, time, place, and purpose of the party. Include a way to RSVP (let you know if they will attend) by a certain date.

6. Glue the white paper to the back of the invitation.

Come to My
Pizza Party

Where ....
Date...............
Time...............

Please RSVP!

Aida had all of the qualities that Verdi sought in a story: passion, courage, loyalty, and patriotism. The work demonstrated Verdi's enormous skillfulness; *Aida* was a grand spectacle. It contained all the basics of traditional grand opera but went far beyond what the composer had accomplished before. The pageantry, the scenery, the ballets, the choral numbers, and the arias of *Aida* are outstanding examples of Verdi's tremendous resourcefulness. The composer blended the text and the music using recurring themes and rich orchestral coloring to effectively convey the exotic splendor of ancient Egypt.

The opera contains magnificent music depicting a love triangle. It tells the story of Aida, an Ethiopian princess, who is captured and brought to Egypt, where she serves as a slave to the Princess Amneris, who does not know her slave's real identity. Radames, an officer in the Egyptian army, is secretly in love with Aida. Complicating this situation is the fact that Princess Amneris also loves Radames and is jealous of his feelings for her slave. Aida is torn between her love for Radames and her love of Ethiopia and her father, King Amonasro.

The score conveys the tragic situation set in an ancient civilization of long ago. *Aida*, although it is still a **number opera** (the various parts are distinct from one another), possesses more continuity than any of Verdi's previous works. The composer used recurring themes and Egyptian musical themes to establish the exotic impression of the music.

Verdi had decided not to travel to Egypt for the premiere, so he completed the orchestration of the opera in Italy. As the details of the opera were finalized for the composer and his librettist, the costumes and scenery were being prepared for transportation to Egypt from France. The outbreak of the Franco-Prussian War interrupted their plans. The Prussians

THE FRANCO-PRUSSIAN WAR

Under the leadership of Prime Minister Otto von Bismarck the Prussians provoked a war with France over the unification of the German states into one country. The French wanted to retain their influence over the German states, which the Prussians now wished to control. The German states were divided over religion, politics, and cultural issues but were united in their hatred of France that had been aroused by the Napoleonic Wars. In July 1870 the French declared war against Prussia.

The Germans falsely depicted France as the aggressor in this new war, causing the southern German states to quickly join the North German Confederation. By August 1870 the Prussians had crossed the border into France and had started to march toward Paris. In September the emperor Napoleon III and 100,000 men of his army were captured. The Prussians surrounded Paris and placed the city under a siege. The people of Paris suffered through months of famine that lasted until January 28, 1871, when an armistice was signed. A united Germany was proclaimed under the Prussian emperor Wilhelm I.

L'HOMME A LA BOULE PAR DRANER.

This cartoon of the Franco-Prussian War shows Kaiser Wilhelm as an acrobat having difficulty balancing on a globe. Library of Congress LC-USZ62-21823

put Paris under a blockade; the scenery and costumes for *Aida* could not be shipped out of the city. The premiere in Cairo had to be postponed. *Aida* finally debuted on December 24, 1871. At its opening the opera was hailed as a world event and became one of the most famous in opera history.

Verdi Versus Wagner

After an Italian premiere of *Aida* at La Scala in 1872, Verdi returned to his estate. World famous and the recognized master of Italian opera, he felt that he had reached the peak of his career. At this time, German operatic music was making inroads in Italy; this development distressed Verdi greatly. Verdi believed that this was an invasion from a foreign culture into what the composer felt was the sacred ground of Italian opera. German opera and Italian opera were locked into a battle between the styles.

The German composer Richard Wagner and Verdi, who were born in the same year but never met, were rivals competing for audiences and style dominance. Their techniques

Music Note: WHAT IS A LEITMOTIF?

A leitmotif is a brief musical theme established to symbolize or represent a particular main character, emotion, place, or object. The word is derived from the German for "lead **motif**." It may be considered a "theme song" or a "signature tune." The recurring musical theme gives the listeners a clue that something specific is happening in the drama. Richard Wagner called these themes "melodic moments." He employed this system to track the components in his operas. Other composers imitated the leitmotif method in their works. It is also a system used in literature and film to symbolize something associated with a character, a setting, or an event.

A leitmotif from the movie Jaws ("Shark Theme") Courtesy of Susan Silberman

and subjects were quite different. The fans of each composer fostered the dispute, which often turned into a heated debate. Verdi and his admirers feared that the direction of future Italian opera composition was coming under the influence of Wagner who had made a tremendous impact on German opera.

Based on German folklore and mythology, Wagner's operas glorified Germanic history. He had developed several techniques that he employed in his works. These techniques included continuous drama without interruption, and a systematic use of motives called leitmotifs ("leading motives") which were a recurring musical theme. Wagner lessened the use of the aria, replacing it with **arioso**, a free lyrical passage that is not as organized as an aria, and extended orchestral segments.

In contrast, Verdi chose realistic human dramas for his operas as opposed to the mythology, symbolism, magic, and hidden messages of Wagnerian opera. He never employed a system of leitmotifs or the symbolism that Wagner used. Verdi sought a simpler, more straightforward approach. He feared that Wagner's compositional methods and style of opera would pollute the Italian operatic heritage. In a letter written years later, Verdi's words clearly expressed his thoughts, "Our young Italians are not patriots. If the Germans, basing themselves

German composer Richard Wagner.
Shutterstock

RICHARD WAGNER

Wilhelm Richard Wagner (1813–1883) was born in Leipzig, Germany, the ninth child in the family. After seeing a production of Beethoven's opera *Fidelio* the youngster requested music lessons. Wagner was taught piano and music theory for about six months; however, for the remainder of his youth he studied music on his own.

His personal life was controversial; his early days were spent escaping debt collec-tors. Later in his life, many of his extreme viewpoints caused concern. Besides his 13 operas, Wagner wrote books and articles that displayed his radical politics and anti-Semitic rants. The lasting controversy and shadow over Wagner was caused by the fact that his "Germanic ideals" became a powerful symbol in the Nazi era during the 20th century.

Many of Wagner's musical concepts were innovative and brilliant. He felt that opera had to be a synthesis of all its components. His vision of "unending melody" caused his music to continuously stream throughout the work without interruption. Wagner believed that every note and chord had to be justifiable; he held that the music and the text had to blend together with the dramatic purpose of the opera. His concepts transformed opera; he was one of the most influential musicians of the 19th century.

on Bach, have culminated in Wagner they act like good Germans, and it is well. But we, the descendents of Palestrina, commit a musical crime in imitating Wagner, and what we are doing is useless, not to say harmful."

Time for Other Interests

AT THE age of 58, Verdi decided to retire from composition and concentrate on his estates and charities since he no longer needed to work and had no financial worries. His apprehensions about the influence of foreign operatic traditions remained a concern that he mentioned on many occasions, but now he wanted to focus his attention on his other interests. For many years after *Aida* he did not compose another opera.

Life at Sant'Agata was peaceful, and Verdi was content. His daughter Maria graduated from school and married her sweetheart, Alberto Carrera, in 1878. One year later his first grandchild, named Giuseppina for her grandmother, was born.

In 1873 a beloved Italian patriot, poet, and novelist died. Alessandro Manzoni's writings were considered masterpieces of Italian literature; the entire country was enshrouded in deep mourning by this loss. Verdi, a lifelong admirer of Manzoni, had been introduced to the poet by his friend Clara Maffei in 1868.

Too overcome by grief to attend the funeral, the composer decided to come out of retirement to write a Requiem Mass to honor and memorialize Manzoni on the first anniversary of the poet's death.

The decision to compose a religious work took Verdi's wife and friends by surprise. The composer had made it clear to them over the years that he was not a religious man; in fact Strepponi was convinced that her husband was an agnostic (someone who questions religious beliefs). She had written to a friend that she suspected that her husband was, "I won't say an atheist, but certainly not much of a believer."

Verdi arranged to have the *Requiem* performed at a Catholic church in Milan. He would conduct it himself. By April the mass was completed and Verdi had selected the soloists; the following month rehearsals began. Like his operas, this religious work showcased his ability to set a text to music that drew out its emotions and images. The stirring *Requiem*, filled with thunderous sounds of the drums and the warning calls of trumpets, was a splendid achievement.

Its first performance was in the church of San Marco, followed by a presentation three days later in the Milan opera house where it received a triumphant reception. Then the *Requiem* began a tour of Europe. Always active in charitable causes, the composer also directed another performance of this work to aid the victims of a flood that had devastated several Italian provinces in 1879.

If Verdi had never composed another work, the *Requiem* would have been a fitting conclusion to his career. Verdi's esteem rose internationally as his latest musical composition was displayed to the world. In 1875, the government of Italy, proud of the achievements of its native son, had declared Verdi a senator for life. He could now finally retire and enjoy his later years. But when, at the end of the decade, the basis for a new opera was suggested to Verdi—he was interested. ❧

FINALE: GREAT MUSIC AND GOOD WORKS

1880–1901

"The artist must look into the future, perceive new worlds amid the chaos."

—Giuseppe Verdi

An engraving of William Shakespeare from *The Leisure Hour* magazine, April 1864.

ONE EVENING IN 1879 Verdi and Giuseppina were seated at a dinner with his publisher Giulio Ricordi when the subject of a new opera arose. Having worked with and printed Verdi's scores over the years, Ricordi was aware of the composer's admiration of Shakespeare. He mentioned the idea of using the play *Othello* as the basis for an opera. "At the mention of *Othello* I saw Verdi look at me with suspicion but with interest. He had certainly understood and had certainly reacted," the publisher reported.

An 1884 Poster for Shakespeare's Othello *featuring the famous American Shakesperean actor Thomas W. Keene.*

Library of Congress LC-USZC6-58

Wooing Verdi

THE LIBRETTO for *Otello* (the Italian version of the title) had already been sketched out by Arrigo Boito, a composer, poet, and novelist. When Boito brought the material to Verdi, the composer was not ready to commit himself to the project. He responded to the sketch by telling the librettist to continue working on it, "for you, for me, for someone else." Hoping the grouchy composer would relent, Boito kept working on the text, just in case.

The composer was occupied with reworking the ballet in *Aïda* to suit the French taste for a performance at the Paris Opéra scheduled for March 1880. While Verdi was altering *Aïda*, Boito arrived at Sant'Agata with his completed *Otello* libretto. Again, Verdi would not commit to writing the music, but he did buy the text from Boito.

Verdi was reluctant to take on the composition of a new opera because he had not composed anything besides the *Requiem* for a great length of time. He was 67. Much had changed

WILLIAM SHAKESPEARE

Considered the greatest and best known English poet and playwright, William Shakespeare (1564–1616) was born in the market town of Stratford-Upon-Avon. He was the oldest son of John and Mary Arden. At 18 Shakespeare married Anne Hathaway, a 26-year-old farmer's daughter. In the first three years of their marriage they had a daughter followed by fraternal twins. In the late 1580s Shakespeare left his family in Stratford and went to London seeking employment.

He worked as an actor and playwright before opening a theater as a partner with other actors in 1599. The Globe Theater was a circular building, three stories high, that could seat 3,000 people. The first play produced there was Shakespeare's *Julius Caesar*.

Shakespeare's poems and plays have been translated into almost every language. His writings are read, performed, and studied by scholars and students all over the world. His plays are categorized as comedies, histories, or tragedies. Also known as the Bard of Avon (bard means poet), Shakespeare's literary works include 38 plays and many poems.

in the opera world, and Verdi feared that he was out of touch with what audiences of the time wanted. Ricordi came up with a plan to make the hesitant composer display an interest in *Otello*. The publisher got Verdi and the librettist together to revise other operas. He also gently nudged Verdi by sending him Christmas gifts of pastries decorated with the image of Shakespeare's Moor of Venice, the title of the main character in the play. Ricordi hoped to capitalize on Verdi's love of Shakespeare.

Verdi took his time before agreeing to this project. It was his second work based on Shakespeare and his last tragedy. The composer had seen Boito's sketches for the opera in the autumn of 1879; by the summer of 1880 he was sent the libretto. The librettist continued to revise the text and waited for Verdi's response until the spring of 1884. Seven years passed before Verdi finally decided to compose the music. By the time he completed scoring the opera in the autumn of 1886, after much sweet-talking and coaxing from the librettist, Verdi was 73.

The first act of Shakespeare's *Othello* was not included in the four-act opera but the remainder closely follows the play. The dramatic music of the opera heightens the tragedy of the story. Although the score displays most of the traditional aspects of Verdi's earlier works, *Otello* exhibits some changes in the composer's style.

A performance of Otello *in Ukraine (May 2011).*

Igor Bulgarin/Shutterstock

The libretto contained continuous action, which required the music to be uninterrupted and fluid. The composer employed what is known as the "kiss motif" to indicate that Otello is thinking about his wife. The **motif** is first heard in the love duet that ends the first act and returns twice more: when Otello kills his wife and in the closing scene of Otello's death. The motif unites the opera from its beginning to its end.

The kiss motif from **Otello.** Courtesy of Susan Silberman

Once *Otello* was completed, the composer insisted that he had to have total control over its production. Verdi was 74 years old when he put together the first performance. He realized that the standards had changed since *Aida* had premiered. In the 1880s the ornate bel canto was out of fashion and opera singers were expected to be able to act out the parts, not just to sing. As the composer considered the cast of *Otello* he thought about the available sopranos. He stated, "If [the candidates] sing ill, no matter! All the better, in fact—they will sing the more readily as I want them to."

A reporter from the New York newspaper the *Daily Telegraph* documented that the pre-

THE WORK OF A CONDUCTOR

Until the middle of the 19th century, composers generally conducted their own music. As the size of orchestras became larger and scores became more complex, the need for someone specialized on the podium to lead the musicians increased. A modern conductor is in charge of all the musical aspects of a production. Often they are the ones to select the works that will be performed. They convey their knowledge about and interpretation of the music to the performers. The conductor makes sure that the musicians are working together while blending their sounds well. Every conductor has his or her own technique for communicating with the ensemble.

During rehearsals the performers further learn what the specific movements made by the conductor mean. He or she uses a baton or their hands to signal the musicians about the tempo, **dynamics** (volume), cueing, and phrasing. The facial expressions and body language of the conductor add another dimension to the performers' understanding of the conductor's expectations. Some conductors send their messages with their entire body. Bending down may mean "play it smoothly" while jumping up on the podium likely indicates the need for some extra excitement to be expressed by the instruments.

miere of *Otello* was postponed by the composer due to details regarding the performance. Verdi was attentive to every aspect regarding the work; he coached and rehearsed with the tenor in the title role until he was satisfied that the singer was totally prepared. Finally Verdi decided the opera was ready.

On February 5, 1887, the seats at La Scala were filled by notable people from all over Italy; critics and journalists came from around the world for the debut. *Otello* was greeted by an adoring public and the audience gave the composer over 20 curtain calls to applaud him. The *New York Times* music critic called the orchestration "one bright jewel of musical art."

From the clashing sounds of the opening storm scene until its heartrending conclusion, *Otello* was carefully crafted. It was a fitting climax for Verdi's tragic works. The famous conductor Arturo Toscanini was a young musician who played second cello at the premiere performance of the work at La Scala. Thrilled by the power of the opera, Toscanini observed, "*Otello* is a masterpiece. Go on your knees, Mother, and say 'Viva Verdi.'"

Comedy and Charity

Otello WENT on to open in major opera houses throughout Europe. Verdi received many honors for his latest work, including being made an honorary citizen of Milan. The money that *Otello* earned allowed him to finish a project that he had started in 1882. This project had grown out of the composer's concern for the farm workers and their families who lived in the villages surrounding him. There was no local hospital and these people had to journey to a distant city for medical care. Verdi designed and paid for a hospital to be constructed in the nearby town of Villanova d'Asti, but he did not allow the facility to be named after him.

This charitable project was completed during a time when Verdi was saddened by the death of his friend Clara Maffei, with whom he had corresponded for many years. As she was dying he interrupted a vacation to visit her in Milan. Before he left the city, the directors of La Scala suggested that he write a comic opera. Verdi jokingly asked them if they knew his age and spoke of his desire to live a simple life at Sant'Agata.

But the idea of writing a comic opera remained in his thoughts. The composer weighed the possibilities; his age and health concerned him. Although he seemed to be feeling fine, would he have the stamina and energy to compose and oversee another work? Boito urged the composer to consider Shakespeare's plays *The Merry Wives of Windsor* and *Henry IV* as the basis for a comic work. In 1889 the librettist

ITALIAN TOMATO SAUCE

Tomatoes were first brought to Europe by Spanish soldiers and explorers returning from South America during the 16th century. The high acid content in tomatoes caused the pewter plates, used at the time, to leach out lead and make people ill with lead poisoning, so the fruit was feared and its nutritional value questioned. In 1790 Francesco Leonardi, a Neapolitan chef, published a cookbook containing tomato sauce recipes. It took a few more years for the tomato to become a staple in Italian kitchens. In 1810 an Englishman patented the tin can, allowing the eventual mass canning of the processed tomatoes for sale to the public.

Italians began to make sauce out of tomatoes to top their pasta dishes. It was a perfect combination with the small breads that became pizza. The popularity of the red sauce, closely associated with Italian cooking, spread wherever Italians migrated. Many people grow tomatoes in their backyards to enjoy in salads and as an ingredient in homemade sauce.

sent a draft of this opera (named for the Shakespearean character Falstaff) to Verdi that he immediately liked. In response the composer invited Boito to come to see him during a vacation in the Tuscan town of Montecatini Terme, a place famous for its thermal baths, health spas, hotels, and excellent restaurants. Tuscan cuisine is known for its use of fresh, locally grown ingredients.

Verdi, although intrigued by the prospect of composing a comic opera based on Shakespeare, continued to have doubts. Years before, during an interview, Verdi had declared that he would only write a comic opera if the libretto made him laugh first. *Falstaff* had fulfilled that requirement. He wrote to Boito,

> *In outlining* Falstaff *did you never consider the extreme number of my years? I know you will reply exaggerating the state of my health, which is good, excellent, robust. . . . So be it but in spite of that you must agree that I could be accused of being very rash in taking on this work!*

Boito countered the argument with a quote from *A Sentimental Journey* by Laurence Sterne: "a smile can add a thread to the very short texture of life." Verdi wrote back agreeing to compose the opera.

In 1890 a newspaper in Milan wrote a headline announcing "A New Opera by Giuseppe Verdi." The public was astonished; the 77-year-old **maestro** was working again!

Meanwhile Verdi took on another philanthropic project. He was going to build a rest home in Milan for elderly opera singers and musicians. Verdi bought the land in 1889, paid for and supervised construction of the palazzo, a grand building, set in beautiful surroundings. The architect of the facility was Camillo Boito, the brother of his librettist. Today, the Casa di riposo per Musicisti (Home of Repose for Musicians), known as Casa Verdi, remains a retirement home for poor, retired musicians.

Plant a "Tomato Sauce" Garden

A SIMPLE but tasty tomato sauce requires only a few ingredients; tomatoes grown in your own garden or a container will add additional flavor to the dish. Keep in mind the size of the space in which you will place your plants when you pick the variety of tomato to grow. Select plants with thick stems and healthy green leaves. Tomato plants need full sun exposure for most of the day; they can only be grown during a summer-like season (unless you have a greenhouse).

You'll Need

- ∞ Tomato plants
- ∞ Shovel or trowel
- ∞ Garden spot or container with a drainage hole
- ∞ Potting soil (for a container)
- ∞ Water
- ∞ Fertilizer
- ∞ Plant stakes or tomato cages

1. With a shovel or trowel remove some soil in the garden or container to make a space to place the roots and about 30 percent of the plant stem.

2. Moisten the soil with some water (do not make it muddy), and gently place a plant into the hole. It is OK to bury some of the lower leaves.

3. Cover the buried stem with soil, making sure the remainder of the plant stands upright.

4. Add the fertilizer according to the directions on its package.

5. Stake the plants as they grow. Keep the soil moist, remove any weeds, and check the stakes every few days. Fertilize the plants once a week (following the manufacturer's directions).

6. Your tomatoes are ready to pick when the entire fruit has turned red (or yellow for yellow varieties). Use them in the following recipe to make a simple sauce.

Adult supervision required

Tomato Sauce
¼ cup olive oil
6 chopped tomatoes
3 chopped onions
2 cloves garlic
salt and pepper to taste

In a large saucepan, heat the oil over medium heat. Add the tomatoes, onions, garlic, and seasonings; stir the ingredients. Cover the pan; turn the heat to low, and let the sauce simmer for 30 to 45 minutes. Serve over your favorite pasta.

Makes six ½-cup servings.

Casa Verdi, a rest home for musicians in Milan, Italy. Shutterstock

Verdi wrote to a friend,

Of all my works, that which pleases me the most is the home that I had built in Milan to shelter elderly singers who have not been favored by fortune, or who, when they were young, did not have the virtue of saving their money. Poor and dear companions of my life!

The composer insisted that he and his wife were to be buried there. In his will he left a sizable amount of money plus all of the future royalties from his operas to the facility.

These projects consumed a large portion of Verdi's time while he was composing his final opera. By March 1890, Boito had sent the composer the third and last act of the text; this time Verdi would not leave the orchestration undone until rehearsals began as he had done many times in the past. Worried that his health would prevent him from completing this commitment, Verdi continually worked on *Falstaff*, even making small changes on opening night. He attacked the score with an intensity that belied his seeming outward calmness. Almost finished with the work he wrote, "It's true that as I get older I am growing quiet, patient, good-tempered, calm … that won't keep me from the exceptional moment of obstinate fury, worse still than of old. Look out!" During the last month of 1892 *Falstaff* was completed.

Verdi began casting the opera while others completed the preparations for its premiere. Stage sets had to be planned and constructed, costumes designed and sewn, lighting and props and all the details to present a new work needed attention. Once the singers for the main characters had been chosen, rehearsals could begin.

Set in Windsor, England, during the 15th century, *Falstaff* combines the Shakespearean comedy *The Merry Wives of Windsor* with scenes from the historical *Henry IV*. The opera takes place during a single day; it begins in the Garter Inn and ends in Windsor Park. Only seven bars of loud music introduce the action, which rapidly unfolds.

The plot opens as Sir John Falstaff, a stout, scheming knight, comes up with a plan to enrich himself by writing identical letters to Alice Ford and Meg Page, two wealthy, married women, offering them his love. The women receiving the letters immediately recognize his dishonesty and decide to teach him a lesson. All of the conspirators, most dressed in costumes to hide their identities, are waiting at the park to confront the knight. The comedy ends with a final fugue in which Falstaff and the other characters declare "the world is but a joke."

In 1893 *Falstaff* premiered at La Scala. Verdi was almost 80. *Falstaff* displays the composer at the peak of his powers; it is a technical masterpiece. The inventive melodies, brilliant orchestration, and complete integration of the text with the music make the opera a wonderful achievement, especially considering Verdi's age at the time of its composition. The comic work brought out his inventiveness as well as his sense of humor and playfulness. The music

Verdi conducting rehearsals for **Falstaff.**

From *L'Univers illustré*, 1894, courtesy of Bibliothèque nationale de France

OPERA PRODUCTION

In order to produce an opera many people with various skills and talents must work together under the guidance and supervision of the conductor and **stage director.** Just as the conductor is in charge of all of the musical aspects, the **stage director** helps to plan and oversee all the people involved in the various aspects of the production. In world-famous opera houses the director may lead a production management team responsible for coordinating the artistic and business aspects of the opera. Together the director and the team ensure that everything comes together on time and within the established budget.

Dozens of people are involved in the presentation of an opera. A large opera house employs people who design sets, costumes, props, wigs, and makeup. They may also have lighting and technical experts plus electricians, carpenters, seamstresses, and wardrobe managers on their staff. Teams work closely together to plan and execute each phase of production, often meeting with one another and the director to coordinate all the details. Each element of the production adds a layer to the enjoyment of the work, enhancing and intensifying the experience for the audience.

Sketch a Costume Design for Falstaff

MANY OF the characters in *Falstaff* wear disguises in the second scene of the third act. Dressed in fairy costumes, actors pinch and poke the title character. Designing clothing for this scene requires your imagination. Try your hand at designing these fairy costumes.

You'll Need

- ∞ The libretto for act 3, scene 2 of *Falstaff* (available in a book or online)
- ∞ Scratch paper
- ∞ Pencil
- ∞ Sketch paper
- ∞ Crayons or markers
- ∞ Fabric samples (available at fabric stores)

1. Read the libretto containing the scene several times until you have a clear image of it in your mind. Think about what costume would make the audience think they were seeing a fairy.

2. Make notes about what the costumes should be made out of. Start with the head covering and work down to the shoes. What fabrics would you use for the head coverings? What fabrics would you use for the costumes? What kind of shoes would work? Should the actors be holding something like a wand?

3. Sketch out your ideas for the fairy costumes.

4. Color in the sketches.

5. Note the fabrics and accessories needed to complete the costumes on the sketches. For a professional-looking sketch, attach swatches of the fabrics you suggest to your drawings.

responds to the text's witty tone. Its rhythms, colors, textures, and harmonies capture the cheerfulness of the lighthearted comedy. In his letters and interviews following the debut of *Falstaff* the composer explained, "In writing *Falstaff* I haven't thought about either theaters or singers. I have written for myself and my own pleasure."

Falstaff was the perfect opera to end Verdi's compositional career. Although after this opera he never again composed anything for the stage, Verdi did write four sacred pieces, including one to benefit the victims of an earthquake. He wrote these religious works as a tribute to the Italian culture that produced giants such as the Renaissance composer Giovani Palestrina and the medieval poet Dante Alighieri. The works reflect the concern that Verdi continued to have regarding Italian cultural integrity and unity. In 1897, Verdi sent these pieces to his publisher just before a great tragedy befell him.

GIANTS OF ITALIAN CULTURE

GUIDO D'AREZZO (c. 990–c. 1050) A musical monk and music theorist who developed the musical staff.

MARCO POLO (c. 1254–1324) The first European to travel to the Far East.

DANTE ALIGHIERI (1265–1321) Author and philosopher; writer of *The Divine Comedy,* a masterpiece of Renaissance literature.

LEONARDO DA VINCI (1452–1519) Artist, architect, and engineer of the Renaissance, famous for his paintings and scientific studies.

NICCOLÒ MACHIAVELLI (1469–1527) Best known for his pamphlet *The Prince*, which provides an explanation of the power of the nobility.

MICHELANGELO BUONARROTI (1475–1564) Artist, architect, and poet of the Renaissance, considered one of the greatest artists in history.

GALILEO GALILEI (1564–1642) Scientist, mathematician, astronomer, and philosopher, called the Father of Modern Science.

GUGLIELMO MARCONI (1874–1937) The electrical engineer and inventor is called the Father of Modern Communications. Won the Nobel Prize in Physics in 1909 for his system of transmitting wireless signals.

ENRICO FERMI (1901–1954) Physicist was awarded the Nobel Prize in 1938 for his discovery of nuclear fission. Together with J. Robert Oppenheimer he is known as the Father of the Atomic Bomb.

Final Years

IT SEEMED that the composer was facing his last days when one morning in January 1897 Giuseppina found him lying in his bed unable to move. He was paralyzed and could not speak, but he motioned that he needed a pen and paper. With a trembling hand Verdi wrote "coffee." Amazingly, within a few days the symptoms had disappeared.

Later that year Giuseppina passed away, at the age of 82. Her funeral was held in the Busseto church, and she was buried in a Milan cemetery. Verdi was filled with sadness. He wrote

An elderly Verdi and guests at Sant'Agata, c. 1898. Seated from left to right: Verdi's adopted daughter, Maria Carrera; sister-in-law Barberina Strepponi; Verdi; and Giuditta Ricordi (wife of Giulio Ricordi). Standing from left to right: singer Teresa Stolz, lawyer Umberto Campanari, publisher Giulio Ricordi, and composer Metlicevik.

to his friend, "Great sorrow does not demand great expression; it asks for silence, isolation, I would even say the torture of reflection."

Depressed and alone in the rural setting of Sant'Agata, the composer soon decided to move into the Grand Hotel in Milan. He kept himself occupied overseeing the final details of the construction of the musicians' rest home.

He made certain that when the time came, he would be buried on its grounds. During his final four years Verdi had many visitors come to see him. Journalists had questions to ask, musicians sought his advice and approval, and friends just wanted to spend time with him.

On January 21, 1901, the composer had a stroke. Crowds of people gathered in front of the

Verdi's funeral, February 27, 1901.

Lebrecht Music & Arts Photo Library, Photographers Direct

hotel after hearing the news. They were hoping for his recovery and waiting to learn more about his condition. Even the streets beneath his windows were covered with straw so that the traffic noises would not disturb his rest.

The composer passed away six days later. The *New York Times* reported that his funeral was a simple ceremony held at the Church of Saint Francis. He had not wanted flowers, so his daughter and granddaughter gently placed palm fronds in his coffin. A banner hanging in front of the church read PEACE TO THE SOUL OF GIUSEPPE VERDI. He was temporarily buried until a state funeral was organized.

On February 27 the state funeral took place; 200,000 people attended. Verdi and Giuseppina's coffins were moved to a crypt built on the grounds of the musicians' retirement home. Arturo Toscanini conducted a full orchestra and a choir of 800 voices in performing "Va, pensiero," the chorus from *Nabucco*. The huge crowd spontaneously joined in the singing as the hearse drawn by horses passed them.

Verdi's legacy includes his efforts to unite the country he loved, the charities he created, and his concern for others less fortunate. His operas dominated the Italian opera world for most of the 19th century. From his first triumphs to *Falstaff*, his melodic gift, technical abilities, understanding of human passions, and grasp of what created great theater caused his immense popularity. He composed his works carefully, stating, "I do not write my notes at random but try to give them a definite character." ❧

ACKNOWLEDGMENTS

ONCE AGAIN, I would like to thank the entire staff at the Chicago Review Press for their expert guidance and attention to detail; they bring meaningful and interesting books to young people. Another heartfelt thanks to the artist Susan Silberman, who teaches technology at the Don Estridge High Tech Middle School in Boca Raton, Florida. My gratitude extends to Janice Blumenthal and her third-grade class at Hagen Ranch Elementary in Boynton Beach, Florida, for testing activities. Teachers really do make a difference. Lastly, thanks to Edward Bauer, who always graciously provides me with his computer expertise; without his support and assistance I would be lost in a PC maze.

Opera, in particular Verdi's operas, are enchanting and exhilarating. I will never forget the first time I experienced *Aida* at the Metropolitan Opera in New York City—although I stood with other students throughout the performance at the very top level of the auditorium where the air was quite thin. From the heights of the standing-room-only section in the rear of the tallest balcony I felt myself being elevated higher and higher by the uplifting music.

RESOURCES

Recommended Recordings

Aida

Label: Opera D'oro

This live recording of a La Scala performance features the magnificent voices of Martina Arroyo and Plácido Domingo. There is some slight hissing noise in the background, but the overall quality is very good.

Attila

Label: Opera D'oro

On this CD the energetic music of *Attila* is conducted by the former music director of La Scala, Riccardo Muti. The baritone Ruggero Raimondi is cast in the title role alongside Antonietta Stella singing the part of Odabella. A vibrant performance of this operatic showdown between good and evil.

Falstaff

Label: Ica Classics

Geraint Evans sings the title role and Ilva Ligabue portrays Alice Ford with Vittorio Gui conducting the Royal Philharmonic Orchestra. This recording comes from the famous British Glyndebourne Festival's 1960 season.

Il trovatore

Label: Decca

Luciano Pavarotti, Marilyn Horne, Joan Sutherland, and Ingvar Wixell perform the leading roles in this spirited recording. The National Philharmonic Orchestra and London Opera Chorus are conducted by Richard Bonynge, the husband of Joan Sutherland.

I masnadieri

Label: Opera D'oro

Under the baton of Gianandrea Gavazzeni this live recording of one of Verdi's lesser-known operas is fabulous. Although the work is rarely performed, the lovely melodies and resounding choruses of the work should create more demand for its production.

La battalia di Legnano

Label: Opera D'oro

The tenor Franco Corelli made his debut in *Il trovatore* at New York's Metropolitan Opera. In this recording he is joined by the fine soprano Antonietta Stella and the rich voice of the baritone Ettore Bastianini. The live recording was made at La Scala in 1961.

Macbeth

Label: Deutsche Grammophon

The chorus and orchestra of La Scala are conducted by Claudio Abbado in this powerful performance. The part of Lady Macbeth was sung by the fantastic African American soprano, the late Shirley Verrett.

Nabucco
Label: Decca Records
This two-disc recording was conducted by Lamberto Gardelli, who specialized in Verdi's operas. The soloists and Vienna Opera orchestra and chorus do a superb job on this CD and MP3 download.

Otello
Label: Myto
The wonderful voices of Mario del Monaco (Otello), Renata Tebaldi (Desdemona), and Leonard Warren (Iago) make this live performance sparkle. The 1954 presentation of this work at La Scala had the audience cheering wildly.

DVDs

The Life of Verdi
Kultur Video, 1982; directed by Renato Castellani
This made-for-television miniseries was filmed in many European countries. The music is performed by world-famous opera singers. Available in some libraries, bookstores, and online stores.

Aida
Kultur Video, 1981; directed by Brian Large
Margaret Price and Luciano Pavarotti combine to make this a memorable performance. Directed by Sam Wanamaker at the San Francisco Opera, this is an extraordinary presentation.

Falstaff
Euroarts, 2001; directed by Pierre Cavassilas
This performance features Ambrogio Maestri as Falstaff and Barbara Frittoli as Alice Ford. The costumes and scenery are recreated from a 1913 performance that was conducted in the same theater by Arturo Toscanini to commemorate the 100th anniversary of Verdi's birth.

I Lombardi
Kultur Video, 2004; directed by Brian Large
This 1984 performance at La Scala, with the great tenor voice of José Carreras in the lead role of Oronte, is an exciting production. The sets by Giovanni Agostinucci are as amazing as the voices.

La traviata
Universal Studios, 1982; directed by Franco Zeffirelli
James Levine conducts at the Metropolitan Opera with Teresa Stratas in the role of Violetta and Plácido Domingo as Alfredo. Interesting production notes and cast biographies are included.

Oberto
BBC Opus Arte, 2007; directed by Ignacio Garcia
This DVD of Verdi's first opera presents the Russian bass Ildar Abdrazakov in the title role. He has been in the international spotlight since he won the 2000 Maria Callas International Television Competition.

Rigoletto
Deutsche Grammophon, 2004; directed by Kirk Browning
Plácido Domingo sings the role of the duke at the Metropolitan Opera with James Levine conducting. The DVD includes bonus material with a photo gallery and interviews.

Verdi
Universal Music, 2000; directed by Zubin Mehta
This wonderful recording of some Verdi arias was performed by the tenor Andrea Bocelli and the Israel Philharmonic Orchestra under the direction of Zubin Mehta at the Mann Auditorium in Tel Aviv.

Websites

Giuseppe Verdi (official website)
www.giuseppeverdi.it/ing
A website maintained by the Province of Parma, it features a biography, music samples, pictures, and videos.

A Tribute to Giuseppe Verdi
www.giuseppe-verdi.net
Constructed by an admirer of the composer, this website provides a brief overview of Verdi's life and some of his works.

Stanford University List of Verdi Operas
http://opera.stanford.edu/Verdi/main.html
Provides name of the librettists, the estimated year of completion of each work, and the year and location of each premiere. It also includes a list of recordings.

NOTES

Chapter 1

"May God strike you down" Budden, *Verdi*, 3

"the good disposition" Budden, *Verdi*, 3

"From the ages of" Parker, *The New Grove Guide*, 11

Chapter 2

"Lavigna was very strong" and "He was learned" Budden, *Verdi*, 8

"this most unhappy town" Rosselli, *The Life of Verdi*, 25

"My family has been destroyed" Machlis, *The Enjoyment of Music*, 235

Chapter 3

"I came into my room" Machlis, *The Enjoyment of Music*, 235

"Isn't it beautiful?" Budden, *Verdi*, 20

"One day one line" Budden, *Verdi*, 20

"He shouts like a desperate man" Rosselli, *The Life of Verdi*, 36

Chapter 4

"like living on a steamer" and "they do not suit" Budden, *Verdi*, 44

"Always together at lunch" Budden, *Verdi*, 29

"I have never heard worse singers" Rosselli, *The Life of Verdi*, 63

"Honor to all Italy" Rosselli, *The Life of Verdi*, 78

"You talk of music to me!!" Budden, *Verdi*, 40

"Force still rules the world!" Martin, *Verdi*, 205

"have the whole world" from *Attila*

"As soon as you get this letter" Portland Opera Study Guide for Rigoletto, http://www.portlandopera.org/sites/files/09%20season/09%20education/Rigoletto_study_guide.pdf

"The suspicion that" Weaver, *Verdi*, 180

"The decree refusing" Weaver, *Verdi*, 181

"Putting on the stage" Budden, *Verdi*, 58

"As far as dramatic effectiveness" Werfel and Stefan, *Verdi*, 175

"years in the galley" Budden, *Verdi*, 31

"The public listened" Opera de Oviedo, www.operaoviedo.com

"a subject for our time" Budden, *Verdi*, 62

"In the theater" Machlis, *The Enjoyment of Music*, 238

"Was it my fault" Machlis, *The Enjoyment of Music*, 238

Chapter 5

"Where is the longed for" Budden, *Verdi*, 84

"In my house there lives" Budden, *Verdi*, 60

"We are still the whole world" Budden, *Verdi*, 65

"How beautiful, how elegant" Rosselli, *The Life of Verdi*, 81

"a town where people" Rosselli, *The Life of Verdi*, 81

"I'm in a sea of troubles!" Budden, *Verdi*, 79

Chapter 6

"My head won't stand" Budden, *Verdi*, 84

"The hour of liberation" Rosselli, *The Life of Verdi*, 78

"If you go to India" Rosselli, *The Life of Verdi*, 86

"a peasant from Roncole" Rosselli, *The Life of Verdi*, 12

"Giuseppe Verdi who has" Budden, *Verdi*, 94

Chapter 7

"Let no one else" Rosselli, *The Life of Verdi*, 12

"I am absolutely resolved" Rosselli, *The Life of Verdi*, 122

"I don't know with" Rosselli, *The Life of Verdi*, 122

"It may be that" Budden, *Verdi*, 93

"Our young Italians" Grout, *A Short History of Opera*, 352

"I won't say an atheist" Budden, *Verdi*, 117

Chapter 8

"At the mention" Budden, *Verdi*, 127

"for you, for me" Rosselli, *The Life of Verdi*, 169

"If [the candidates] sing" Rosselli, *The Life of Verdi*, 177

"one bright jewel" Stanford Opera, http://opera.stanford.edu/Verdi/Otello/history.html

"*Otello* is a masterpiece" San Diego Opera notes, Sdopera.com

"In outlining *Falstaff*" and "a smile can add" Budden, *Verdi*, 136

"Of all my works" Lubrani. *Verdi*, 82

"It's true that as" Rosselli, *The Life of Verdi*, 181

"In writing *Falstaff*" Parker, *The New Grove Guide*, 230

"Great sorrow" Budden, *Verdi*, 146

"I do not write" Budden, *Verdi*, 158

GLOSSARY

MANY OF THESE words are used in any conversation about music or the theater, but others relate specifically to opera. Much of the vocabulary surrounding opera comes from Italian, German, or French because many of the early composers came from the countries in which those languages were spoken.

act a main division of an opera. A portion of the dramatic structure of the work which have a climax of its own.

aria the most elaborate lyrical song for a solo voice.

arioso a short passage in the middle or at the end of a *recitative*.

baritone the middle male voice.

bel canto Italian phrase meaning "beautiful singing"; also refers to operas written in this style.

chorus a group of vocalists singing together.

coloratura a type of soprano with a high range who can execute the style of singing that involves elaborate *ornamentation* and *embellishment*.

comic opera a work of an amusing nature.

composer the person who writes the music for the opera.

conductor the person who leads the orchestra and singers; sometimes called the *maestro*.

diva used to describe a female opera star; the literal translation is "goddess."

duet a musical piece for two singers.

dynamics The degree of loudness in music.

ensemble a group of musicians who perform as a unit.

finale the last musical number of an opera or the last number of an act.

flat a note played a semitone (half a tone) lower than it would otherwise be played.

impresario the person who sponsors or produces entertainment, such as the director of an opera company.

interlude a short piece of instrumental music played between scenes or acts.

key the specific tonality of a piece of music, indicating the precise pitch that serves as the tonal center.

key signature indicates the key or the tone in which the music was written. It tells you which notes will be sharp or flat.

leitmotif a musical theme established to represent a particular idea or main character.

libretto the written text for an opera; the script.

librettist(s) the writer who creates or adapts an operatic text before it is set to music.

maestro a master; used to describe a great composer, conductor, or teacher of music.

melodrama a dramatic text, characterized by extravagant theatricality, intense plot and action.

melody the tune of the music.

mezzo-soprano the middle female voice.

motif a short musical idea.

natural A note without a flat or sharp symbol.

number opera an opera in which the individual arias, ensembles, recitatives, and other sections are clearly separated from one another.

opera Italian meaning "the work;" a libretto sung and acted to an instrumental accompaniment.

opera buffa Italian for "comic opera."

orchestra the group of instrumentalists.

orchestration the art of writing for the orchestra.

ornamentation the addition of extra notes, such as trills, to an already-established melody line; also called *embellishment.*

overture the orchestra's introduction to a larger work.

pit the sunken area in front of the stage where the members of the orchestra play.

pitch the accuracy of the musical notes.

prima donna the principal woman singer in an opera; literally means "first lady" in Italian.

production the entire presentation of the work including the sets, costumes, props, lights, etc.

production management The team responsible for coordinating the artistic and business aspects of the opera, insuring that everything happens on time and within budget.

props the items carried or used by performers on stage; short term for properties.

range the span of notes from lowest to highest that a voice or an instrument can produce.

recitative a form of presenting text using normal speech rhythms with a light accompaniment. The purpose of recitative is to advance the plot.

repertoire or **repertory** the works that a singer or company has ready to present.

scene a portion of an act in which the action takes place in one setting.

score(s) the music used by the conductor; it contains all the music for the orchestra and/or the singers.

sharp a note played a semitone higher than it would otherwise be played.

solo a piece of music written for one voice or instrument.

soprano the highest female voice.

stage director someone who instructs the singers about their onstage movements and the interpretation of their roles.

tempo the speed of the music.

tenor the highest male voice.

theme a tune or subject of an opera.

time signature tells you how many beats are in a measure and which type of note gets one beat.

tonal music in a particular key; a particular pitch or vibration.

BIBLIOGRAPHY

Brown, Sarah, and David O'Connor. *Medieval Craftsmen: Glass-Painters*. London: British Museum Press, 1991.

Budden, Julian. *Verdi*. New York: Oxford University Press, 2008.

Grout, Donald Jay. *A History of Western Music*. New York: W.W. Norton, 1973.

Grout, Donald Jay and Hermine Weigel Williams. *A Short History of Opera*. New York: Columbia University Press, 2003.

Lubrani, Mauro. *Verdi a Montecatini*. Firenze: Polistampa, 2001.

Machlis, Joseph. *The Enjoyment of Music*. New York: W. W. Norton and Company, 1955.

Martin, George. *Aspects of Verdi*. New York: Dodd, Mead & Company, 1988.

Martin, George. *Verdi: His Music, Life and Times*. New York: Dodd. Mead and Company, 1963.

Parker, Roger. *The New Grove Guide to Verdi and His Operas*. New York: Oxford University Press, 2007.

Phillips-Matz, Mary Jane. *Verdi: A Biography*. New York: Oxford University Press, 1993.

Rosselli, John. *The Life of Verdi*. New York: Cambridge University Press, 2006.

Schonberg, Harold. *The Lives of the Great Composers*. New York: W. W. Norton, 1997.

Weaver, William. *Verdi: A Documentary Study*. London: Thames and Hudson, 1977.

Weaver, William and Martin Chusid. *The Verdi Companion*. New York: Norton, 1979.

Werfel, Franz and Paul Stefan, *Verdi: The Man and His Letters*. New York: Vienna House, 1973.

Music Dictionaries

Kennedy, Michael and Joyce Bourne, eds. *The Concise Oxford Dictionary of Music*. New York: Oxford University Press, 1996.

Sadie, Stanley and John Tyrell. *The New Grove Dictionary of Music and Musicians*. London: Macmillan, 2000.

INDEX

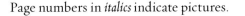

❧